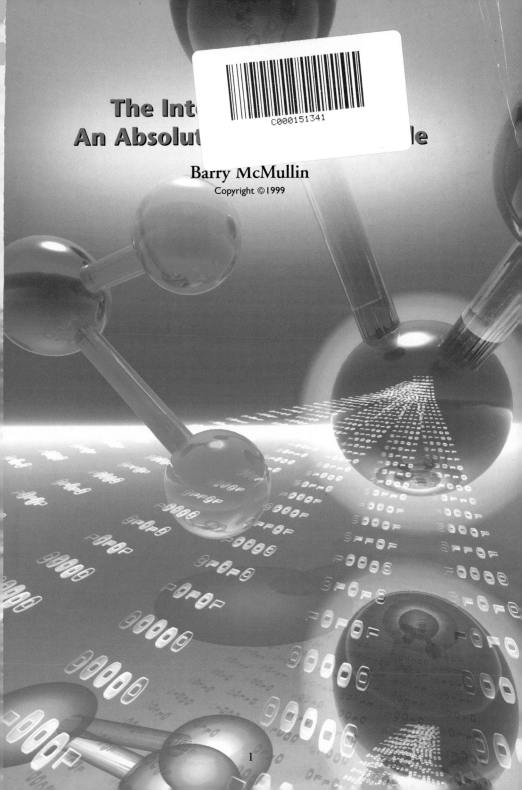

The Inte...
An Absolut...le

Barry McMullin
Copyright ©1999

ABOUT THE AUTHOR

Dr. Barry McMullin is currently Dean of Teaching and Learning at Dublin City University. He has been involved in using, developing, and teaching about Internet technologies for more than 10 years, and has a specific responsibility within DCU for exploring the use of new information and communication technologies in university education. As director of the DCU Artificial Life laboratory, he also leads an internationally recognised research programme on advanced, biologically inspired, computer systems, and acts as a consultant on computer security and communications.

Dr. Barry McMullin

The publishers wish to thank *IOL* as sponsor of this publication.

First Published in the Republic of Ireland in 1999.
Revised and reprinted in December 1999
Revised and reprinted in November 2001

Best Selling Books Ltd.
5/7 Main Street,
Blackrock,
Co. Dublin.

ISBN: 0-9535977-0-9

Author: Barry McMullin.

Design: PML..
Printed By: Brookfield Printing Company Ltd.

The assistance of the Microsoft Corporation is acknowledged by the publisher.

The publishers acknowledge the rights of the trademark holders mentioned in this book.

CONTENTS

Welcome Aboard

Ever since computer technology was invented in the late 1940s it has been surrounded by jargon. Some of this special technical language is very useful. It can make it easier for computer professionals to communicate precisely with each other. But this jargon has also made it very difficult for ordinary people to understand and use computers. Computers are discussed with strange words and seemingly meaningless acronyms - RAM, CPU, CD-ROM, MByte, GUI, and so on. They then appear to be far too complicated for ordinary people to make sense of.

The hype about the *Internet,* the *Web* and the *Information Superhighway* has only made things worse. We see "web addresses" appearing on everything from business cards to breakfast cereal boxes. We have been told that a revolution is underway (leading to the *Information Society* - whatever that is), but it sometimes seems that nobody over the age of about 15 is eligible to join in.

This book is dedicated to the idea that that is all nonsense. There may well be a revolution in progress, but *everybody* is invited, and you don't need a college degree before you start.

Cars, televisions and the international telephone network are all extremely complex technologies, but that does not mean that they can be used only by trained experts. The Internet is not as easy to use as those more established technologies - yet. But it is getting easier to use all the time. Better still, as more people use it, it becomes easier and more useful to each new person who gets connected.

The book explains, step-by-step, and in ordinary language, what the Internet is, what it can do - and what it can't do. I will not be able to avoid jargon completely, though I do try to use as little as possible. Where I have to use it, each technical term will be explained carefully when it is first introduced. I show you how to go about getting "on" the Internet, and how to then use it effectively and enjoyably. I also tell you about some dangers of the Internet and how to avoid them.

I encourage you to read the whole book through before you try to get connected to the Internet at all. Then keep it close by as you follow the step by step hints and instructions. If you do this, you'll be confidently and effectively using the Internet much faster than you might ever have thought possible!

Welcome Aboard

What Is This Internet Thing Anyway

Your Net Computer

Getting On-line

The Web

E-mail

Other Internet Services

Welcome Aboard

What Is This Internet Thing Anyway

Your Net Computer

Getting On-line

The Web

E-mail

Other Internet Services

1. What is this Internet thing anyway?

A computer *network* is a collection of computers connected together so that they can exchange information. Each of the individual computers becomes much more flexible and useful as a result.

The *Internet* is a special kind of computer network. I will explain what is special about it, but first we need to understand a little of the history of how it was created.

Often the computers making up a network are located in the same local area - a school, office, hospital, university etc. In that case the network is called a *local area network* or LAN. Sometimes the network is extended to include computers at separate locations - perhaps connecting a sales office to a manufacturing plant. Then the network is called a wide area network or WAN.

The first computer networks, both LANs and WANs, were private and isolated from each other. They usually belonged to a single organisation. They made the activities of that organisation more efficient. However, when it was necessary to exchange information with other organisations, the private network did not help at all. Instead the information had to be printed out and then retyped for the other computer system, or perhaps stored on a magnetic tape or disk - if the other system could read the same kind of tape or disk, which was often not the case.

The obvious solution to these problems was to *interconnect* these separate networks to form one big network - an "inter-network" or *internet* for short. And that is precisely how the Internet (now with a capital "I"!) came to be born.

The original Internet was an experimental project funded in the 1970s by the *Defense Advanced Research Projects Agency* (DARPA) in the US. In fact, the forerunner of the Internet as we now know it was called ARPANET.

This project explored the technical problems of interconnecting separate computer networks. One particular objective was to make the whole system robust and reliable even if individual communication links or computers were damaged. In fact, this was the chief military interest in the work. It is a tribute to the engineers and scientists who designed the original Internet that it is *still* operating remarkably reliably even though it now has tens of thousands of networks, containing millions of individual computers.

In the early days the Internet was confined to North America and connected a few tens of networks, mainly in universities and government organisations. It offered two main services:

Electronic Mail: or e-mail. This simply means that people can compose letters on their computers and then post them "electronically" to each other. Similarly, each user has an Internet "mailbox" to receive their incoming electronic letters.

This has a few advantages over traditional paper mail. Firstly, you don't need stamps, and you don't have to walk out to the postbox! Secondly, your letter can be delivered within a very short time of posting (as little as a few seconds). Finally, it is very easy to send the same letter to lots of people, instead of just one. I will discuss e-mail in much more detail in **Chapter 5**.

Electronic Publishing: The idea here is that you can make information from your computer available to everyone else on the Internet. One of the most common uses of electronic publishing has been among academics - lecturers in universities - allowing them to share their research articles. This provided the motivation for much of the way publishing services have been developed on the Internet, so it is worth explaining this application in detail.

Traditionally, academic researchers have published their work in printed journals. Academic libraries subscribe to many hundreds or even thousands of these journals. When a researcher needs to refer to one of these articles he checks his own university's library first; but if, as is often the case, it does not stock the particular journal, he would have to request a copy of the article by post from the author. Authors receive a number of free copies or "offprints" of their published articles for this purpose. But this whole system is very cumbersome and slow. It can take weeks or even months to get a copy of a needed article.

But wait a moment: most articles and papers are prepared on computers now anyway, before being printed for submission to a journal. Would it not be possible to make this electronic version available for immediate access by anyone who wants it? Well, yes, it *is* possible and that is exactly the idea behind Electronic Publishing!

Once an article is published "electronically", then anybody else can have it copied onto their own computer (via the Internet), and print it out on their local printer. This can be done in a few minutes, regardless of how far distant the computers are from each other, and without requiring the original author to be involved at all.

Welcome Aboard

What Is This Internet Thing Anyway

Your Net Computer

Getting On-line

The Web

E-mail

Other Internet Services

Welcome Aboard

What Is This Internet Thing Anyway

Your Net Computer

Getting On-line

The Web

E-mail

Other Internet Services

The earliest form of electronic publishing on the Internet used a mechanism called *file transfer protocol* or FTP. This has now been largely displaced by a more sophisticated mechanism called *hypertext transfer protocol* or HTTP. HTTP underlies what is now called the World Wide Web. The Web is the collection of all information published electronically, by any mechanism, over the Internet. Fortunately you need not worry about the arcane technicalities of FTP or HTTP. You just need to understand the basic idea that the Web is a system for electronic publishing - a way for you to request all kinds of information, on all kinds of subjects, and to receive it more or less instantaneously.

I will deal with the Web in detail in **Chapter 4**.

Although the Internet started as a research project, with a very limited number of partners involved, other organisations soon wanted to become connected as well. Major expansion of the Internet in the US was funded by the *National Science Foundation*. This eventually allowed the great majority of US universities to connect their own local area networks (LANs) to the Internet.

Similar academic and research networks were simultaneously being constructed in other countries of the world - such as the *Joint Academic Research Network* (JANET) in the UK, and the *Higher Education Authority Network* (HEANET) in Ireland. Initially these separate national networks tended to utilise slightly different and incompatible systems, making it difficult to join them together. But modern academic research usually involves international co-operation. This lack of completely compatible international connection was becoming a significant problem.

By the late 1980s it became clear that these networks would be much more useful if they were interconnected through a single compatible system. Since the US Internet was already the largest and best tested system in use, it was natural that other national networks began to adopt the same basic technologies, and interconnect with it. By the early 1990s the Internet existed as a single global network, interconnecting universities and other research organisations around the world. It was paid for by various national funding agencies, such as the Higher Education Authority in Ireland. It was not yet open to individual members of the general public, nor very widely used by commercial organisations.

The basic underlying technology that unites this global network has the rather cumbersome name of *Transmission Control Protocol/Internet Protocol* or (slightly less of a mouthful) TCP/IP. Fortunately, you need to know almost nothing about the intricacies of TCP/IP in order to actually use the Internet!

The beginnings of more popular interest in the Internet coincided with the development of the *World Wide Web*. The Web introduced two new key facilities on the Internet:

> ***Hyperlinks:*** This is a mechanism whereby one document can be electronically "linked" to another related one. So once you access an initial document it becomes very easy (at the proverbial "touch of a button") to access other related ones. These links can be visualised as connecting together documents all around the world into a single gigantic "spider's web".

> ***Multimedia:*** This simply means that electronically published documents are no longer restricted to be conventional text - characters and words that can be read or printed. Instead, "documents" on the Web can include diagrams, photographs, sounds, animations and even movie clips. This has been done in such a way that every type of document carries a standardised unique label that explains the correct way to "view" it - as text, audio or movie clip etc. - and this labelling scheme can be easily extended at any time to admit new types.

These new facilities were again inspired by the needs of the original Internet users - researchers publishing academic papers. These papers almost always refer to other earlier papers, and frequently need to include diagrams, photographs, or other media. But although the new facilities were inspired by these academic requirements, they have had a much wider effect. Quite suddenly, the Internet could be used in a much easier, more friendly, way. A user did not need to know arcane FTP commands to get a document - they could just "point and click" (point at a link to the document and click a button on their keyboard or mouse). Better still, the "documents" that are electronically published, or exchanged by e-mail, could now be in any kind of medium - text, music, photographs, anything at all. This opened up a much wider range of activities that could be done on the Internet, and triggered an explosion of interest - and an explosion of growth.

Which brings us to the Internet that we know today!

In just the last few years the Internet has very suddenly ceased to be an obscure and private toy for academics in ivory towers. Instead literally millions of ordinary people, and tens of thousands of organisations, from all around the world, have gone "online", by connecting to this global network. The "Net" has become a household word, and a regular subject for debate in magazines, newspapers and on television. People of all ages and all walks of life are using the Internet to exchange letters, postcards, snap shots and even movies. Companies, both long established and aggressive young upstarts, are offering a barrage of news, views, information and fiction, in every conceivable shape and form.

Welcome Aboard

What Is This Internet Thing Anyway

Your Net Computer

Getting On-line

The Web

E-mail

Other Internet Services

Welcome Aboard

What Is This Internet Thing Anyway

Your Net Computer

Getting On-line

The Web

E-mail

Other Internet Services

Many of these inhabitants of "cyberspace" - the users of the Internet - want to sell you something. Others just want to play or to be entertained. Others again are using the Net to fight dictatorship, combat world poverty, or plead for the preservation of the tropical rain forests. The Internet now is all this and more, because it is a magnified image of the diversity of human society and communication across the globe. Whether you just want to search for package holiday bargains, or you intend to bring about World Peace, the Internet will allow you to make immediate contact with the information, the people, and the organisations that can make it happen.

So enough of this history: let's get you connected!

2. Your Net Computer

The vast majority of people using the Internet do so via a computer, and this chapter will be mainly concerned with going about acquiring a suitable machine for the job. But there are a couple of possible ways of exploring the Internet without a computer. Depending on your needs and circumstances, one of these may be appropriate for you, so we'll consider them first.

Time For Coffee?

If you do not already own a suitable computer - or even if you do - it is a very good idea to see the Internet in action before you get connected yourself. If you have a relative, friend or neighbour who already uses the Internet, now would be a good time to drop by and ask for a demonstration. But even if you don't know anybody already on the Net, there is still a way of putting a toe in the water: visit a "CyberCafé".

Don't be put off by the trendy jargon - it is still just a café. What adds the *Cyber* is the availability of computers, already connected to the Internet, right by your coffee table. So for a modest extra charge you can find out whether the Net is really everything it is cracked up to be. There will be friendly staff on hand to help you get started and - if you are *really* lucky - the coffee might be quite nice too!

Alternatively, another innovation beginning to appear in Irish shopping centres and other public places is the *Internet Kiosk*. This typically looks somewhat like a telephone kiosk, but with a form of computer terminal instead of a phone. Again, by paying a charge you will get access to the Internet for some specified period of time.

Cybercafés and Internet Kiosks are quickly springing up all over Ireland. Check your local classified telephone directory under "Internet Services" or "Cyber Cafés" to find one close to you.

For The Technophobic: Internet TV?

It is possible to access the Internet via your good old fashioned television set - albeit with some limitations. An Internet-enabled TV - I'll call it a *Net* TV for short - allows many information sources on the World Wide Web to be displayed via your TV set. You could think of this as a sort of highly sophisticated and improved version of the old *teletext* service. A Net TV can also allow access to e-mail, the other main

Welcome Aboard

What Is This Internet Thing Anyway

Your Net Computer

Getting On-line

The Web

E-mail

Other Internet Services

11

Welcome Aboard

What Is This Internet Thing Anyway

Your Net Computer

Getting On-line

The Web

E-mail

Other Internet Services

Internet service - although this is a little more difficult (a TV doesn't *usually* come with a keyboard!). Net access is likely to become fully integrated into TVs in the future, but for the moment a Net TV is generally realised via a separate "black box" - somewhat like a satellite TV decoder. A recent innovation is for *video game consoles* to support Net access. This is partly to allow game players to compete with each other across the Net, but it also generally supports other, "normal", Net TV usage.

A Net TV must have some way of establishing communication with the Internet. This can't be done using conventional TV channels. TV signals are "broadcast" - sent only one-way, from the TV transmitter to the TV receivers. Internet communication is two-way, so a Net TV needs a separate mechanism for sending information back. This can be done via cable TV networks, but needs the whole network to be upgraded to support it. Alternatively, it can use a telephone connection in addition to the "normal" TV connection.

One drawback of the Net TV idea is that TVs are relatively low quality display devices, compared to standard computer screens. This means that information with fine visual detail, such as *text*, is either difficult to read, or must be displayed in relatively large type, and thus in small sections at a time. More seriously, Net TV's tend to be "closed" or proprietary systems. This means that the most recent software programmes for accessing Internet resources may not be available for them - which in turn may impose some significant limitations on what services or sites can be reached with such a device.

Nonetheless, by not looking like a computer, and by being relatively easy to set up and operate, a Net TV may be an attractive option for many people, certainly as an initial introduction to the Internet.

So What Kind Of Computer?

As I said at the start of the chapter, the vast majority of Internet users do so via conventional computers. So, despite the interesting possibilities of Cybercafés, Internet Kiosks and Net TVs, let's return now to consider selecting a suitable *computer* for Internet access.

If you are buying a new car you have a reasonable chance of understanding what the latest "features" are actually all about - sunroof, electric windows, airbag, whatever - and of weighing up what use they will be to you. You don't have to be a rocket scientist to decide between a saloon and a hatchback, two doors or four. If only it was the same with computers!

So what is the difference between a Celeron and a Pentium III? How many MegaBytes or MegaHertz do you really need? What does MMX mean? What's a "modem"? We are in the Jargon Jungle again, but don't despair: behind that jargon the real features are not *all* that much more complicated than in a motor car. I will provide a quick tour of what you really need to know, but fasten your seat belt: we're going to squeeze 50 years of explosive technological progress into just a few pages - and still keep it understandable. This is one of the more complicated sections of the book, but well worth mastering.

The home computer market is dominated by a general category of computers called "PCs". The term PC was popularised by IBM in the early 1980s when it first started selling the IBM *Personal Computer*. But many other companies quickly began selling machines that were similar to the IBM design, so PC is now used as a general term, regardless of who the particular manufacturer may be. These machines are all "compatible" with each other - they are all able to run the same software, or programs. The major alternative to PCs for home computer use is the Macintosh (Mac) family from Apple Computer Inc., including the iMac or *Internet Mac* range, which has been specifically tailored for Internet usage. Much of the discussion presented here will be applicable equally to both PCs and Macs; however, where more specific detail is required I will generally focus on PCs as the more common case.

The core of any personal computer is the *Central Processing Unit* or CPU. This is like the engine of your car: it's what makes the whole thing "go". There are a number of different popular variations in the design of car engines - petrol, diesel, 12-valve, fuel-injection and so on. The CPUs in personal computers have similar variations, but are referred to by rather obscure trade names made up by the manufacturers. The majority of PCs have CPUs manufactured by the Intel Corporation. Recent models include names such as *Pentium III* and *Celeron*. Fortunately, all you really need to know about these names is that the newer models are generally more "powerful" than the old.

Just as with car engines, the "type" is not the only factor - there is also the "horse-power". With car engines of the same general type you know that the bigger the horse-power then the faster you can travel or accelerate. There is an exact parallel for CPUs: it's called the *clock speed*. Think of a CPU as having a tiny clock inside it - except this clock works at different speeds in different computers. The faster your CPU can "tick" then the faster your computer can "go" (can do the things you ask it to do). Clock speed is measured in "millions of ticks per second". The technical term for this is "Megahertz" and abbreviated to *MHz*. If you are buying a new PC now, it should have a CPU clock speed of at least 600 MHz. Note however, that CPU clock speeds are not directly comparable between completely different types of computer - such as Macs versus PCs.

The next part of the computer to consider is the "information storage" capacity. This is very loosely like the space inside your car - how many "passengers" it can hold. Computer storage is needed to hold your computer programs as well your own

Welcome Aboard

What Is This Internet Thing Anyway

Your Net Computer

Getting On-line

The Web

E-mail

Other Internet Services

information such as e-mail, electronic files, books, magazines, photographs, etc. It might be useful to think of it as a *filing cabinet,* holding different kinds of media - paper, photographs, audio and video tapes, etc. In fact, computers often display little filing cabinet pictures or "icons" to represent their storage facilities.

Another way in which computer storage is like a filing cabinet is that not all of it is accessible instantaneously. You know that if you want to use information from a filing cabinet, you must first find the folder or file you want, then take it out of the cabinet and open it up and spread it out on your desk to read it. You could think of your desk as another, specialised, place which you can use to temporarily hold information while you are actively working on it; whereas the filing cabinet is where you store the bulk of your information for the long term. The same idea applies to computers. Your computer will have a big "filing cabinet" that is used for permanent storage, and a much smaller "desktop" that is used to temporarily open up things, so that they can be actively worked on. The "filing cabinet" is called the hard disk drive and the "desktop" is called the RAM or simply the computer memory. RAM actually stands for *Random Access Memory* - but that is an historical phrase and is no longer very meaningful. Think of it as *Rapid Access Memory* instead: it is much faster to access than the disk storage.

The point of all this is that you need to think about how *big* a filing cabinet, and how *big* a desktop you are going to need in your computer. Information is technically measured by a unit called (believe it or not) a *bit.* This stands for "Binary Digit". One bit is one on/off signal, such as the position of a switch, or a "dot" or "dash" in Morse Code (if you can remember Morse Code!). A collection of eight bits is called a *byte.* One byte corresponds roughly to a single character of writing - a single letter, digit, or punctuation mark. So a printed page, with space for about 4,000 characters would hold 4 KByte (kilo-byte). Computers usually deal with much larger amounts of information, so we use units of about a million bytes denoted by MByte (Mega-byte), or even a thousand million bytes denoted by GByte (Giga-byte).

"More" computer storage capacity (both RAM and disk) is clearly going to be "better". The question is, how much do you realistically need? As with the CPU, this is something of a moving target because the requirements are becoming more demanding all the time. A reasonable minimum these days would be 64 MByte RAM and 4 GByte of hard disk space. Your computer should also have a standard "diskette" or "floppy disk" drive. This has much smaller capacity that the hard disk drive (only 1.44 MByte) - but the disks themselves are removable. They are thus usable for transferring information between computers, for installing new software, and for backing up information from your hard disk (as a precaution against both accidental erasure and actual physical failure of the hard disk!).

Your computer also needs some more obvious components. These are the screen or "monitor", the keyboard, and the "mouse". These components are fairly standard, but you will see variations particularly in the monitor and the electronics associated with it (not surprisingly called the "video" hardware). There are four main elements which may vary here:

Video RAM: Yes, "memory" again. This is used specifically to hold the information that is being displayed on the screen. This affects the performance of the computer in complex and subtle ways, but a reasonable minimum is 1MByte.

Screen Resolution: This is a measure of how well the video and the electronics can cope with displaying very fine detail. It is measured in terms of how many individual little dots or "pixels" the screen picture will be made up of. The minimum is 640 horizontal dots by 480 vertical dots; but you should really look for at least 800 by 600.

Colour Depth: This measures how many distinct colours your display can show. This is measured in the number of *bits* needed to represent the colour of each screen pixel. The most common options are 4, 8, 16 or 24 bits per pixel. You will want support for at least 16 bits per pixel.

Monitor Size: Computer screens, just like TV screens, come with a standard shape (i.e., how much wider they are than higher), and the size is measured by the length of the diagonal. And even in this hi-tech metric world, this is one of the last holdouts for Empire, still being measured in inches. A reasonable size is 15". A 17" monitor is also a good choice - but may add significantly to the cost.

Your computer must have a keyboard and a mouse. The mouse is the little device - about the size of a real mouse - that you move around on your desk to make an arrow or pointer move around on your screen, to point at things. Nowadays, like telephones, keyboards and mice can be bought in all manner of exotic shapes and colours. But also just like telephones, none of these affect their technical functioning!

Next, you must have a special device called a *modulator-demodulator!* This is quite a mouthful, so we just say *modem* instead. The modem connects your computer to the telephone system. In simple terms it can convert any kind of computer information into a series of very short bleeps and clicks - noises on the phone. Of course, the faster these bleeps and clicks go, the faster you can exchange information. This is measured in *kbps* or "kilo bits per second". Look for a rating of 56 kbps; this is also commonly referred to as the V90 standard.

Welcome Aboard

What Is This Internet Thing Anyway

Your Net Computer

Getting On-line

The Web

E-mail

Other Internet Services

A modem can be "external" or "internal" - meaning whether it is a separate little box that sits outside your computer, or is fitted away inside the main computer unit. The internal ones are certainly tidier, and I recommend them. However: if you are a beginner (and why else would you be reading this?) don't try to fit an internal modem yourself - buy a computer with one already fitted, or bring your existing computer along to a dealer to fit it for you.

Now we come to a few features or components that might be considered "optional" in a Net computer. You can certainly access the Internet without them; but equally, you would be missing out on some of the benefits.

First of these is a combination of features collectively called "multimedia". This is a rather vague term, but is intended to mean that your computer can effectively handle different "media" types - such as sounds, images, video etc. - as well as the more traditional textual media. In practice, a multimedia computer has "sound support" and a CD-ROM (or possibly DVD) disk drive. We'll consider these in turn.

"Sound support" is just a technical way of saying the computer can make noises! Sound support is optional because a great deal of the information accessed on the Net is purely visual - text, photographs, etc. On the other hand, more and more audio material is being made available. Computer sound support has a sub-jargon all of its own, but the distinctions between one sound system and another are relatively fine, and I will not go into more detail here.

Most new computers these days are equipped with a *CD-ROM* disk drive - or possibly the newer DVD disk drive. A CD-ROM drive is a device that can accept disks that look like conventional music CDs, but which can contain computer data. DVD is a more recent development, originally to allow storage of *video* as opposed to audio material (and thus compete with, say, VHS tapes for distribution of movies etc.), but which can again be used for storing computer data. DVD disks have much greater capacity than CD. A DVD drive can generally access CD-ROM disks also, but not vice versa.

CD-ROM and DVD disks are "read-only" - that is, you cannot change the data stored on them - so that, they are not an alternative to a hard disk drive for storage of your own data. But because they are relatively cheap to manufacture, and can store large quantities of information, they are very popular for distributing new software applications. Many multimedia applications - which have large information requirements - are available *only* in CD-ROM format. You *must* have a CD-ROM or DVD drive if you want to use any of these. Even applications which do not have multimedia content as such - such as Internet access software - are now generally distributed in CD-ROM form (rather than, say, on diskettes).

Welcome Aboard

What Is This Internet Thing Anyway

Your Net Computer

Getting On-line

The Web

E-mail

Other Internet Services

Welcome Aboard

What Is This Internet Thing Anyway

Your Net Computer

Getting On-line

The Web

E-mail

Other Internet Services

*In fact, you will have noticed that this book is accompanied with a free CD-ROM disk. This contains software and instructions for connection to the Internet via one of Ireland's premier Internet service providers, **IOL**, with your choice of **free** (pay-as-you-go) or **premium** (combined subscription/call charge) services.*

So, while a CD-ROM or DVD drive is not an absolutely essential component of a Net computer, it is certainly very convenient to have one. CD-ROM drives come with different "speed" ratings, measured by comparison with the speed of a normal audio CD: a "times-2", or x2, CD-ROM runs at up to twice the speed of an audio CD player; x12 can go up to 12 times faster and so on. As usual, the faster the better. In a new computer you should look for at least x12 CD-ROM speed.

A printer is another optional - but more or less essential - accessory. You will certainly need it if you want to use your computer for things other than Net access - such as word processing etc. But even for Net use, there will often be materials (e-mail messages and other documents acquired electronically) that you would prefer to have in printed form. So called "ink jet" printers are quite reasonably priced, and provide fast, quiet and high quality printing. They are available in both black and white and colour versions. The colour models are naturally somewhat more expensive - but because so much material on the Internet uses colour, I would encourage you to get a colour printer if possible.

That covers the so-called *hardware* of your computer: the physical bits and pieces that make it up. However, before you can actually put your computer to any practical use, you need one final key component: the *software*.

In general, computer "software" is simply the set of instructions which control its operations - how it sequences its activities, what to do when particular buttons are pressed and so on. Software divides into two kinds: the *Operating System* software, which is always active, and so called *Applications* software, which you start up and stop again to handle particular application tasks - word processing, calculations, accessing the Internet etc. A computer is always supplied with Operating System software installed. It will also usually have some applications software provided, but you may then have to install additional applications for particular purposes, such as Internet Access. I will consider Internet Applications Software in detail in later chapters. For now, let's just deal with the Operating System.

For PC computers, the *de facto standard* Operating System is some version of *Microsoft Windows*, which is conveniently pre-installed on most new PCs. Microsoft Windows continues to develop on an ongoing basis, and you may encounter a variety of slightly different versions - Windows 98, Windows Millenium Edition, Windows XP and so on. However, from a user's point of view there are generally sufficiently similar that once you have learned to use one Windows Operating System you should find little difficulty adusting to another.

Alternatively, in recent years, many experienced computer users have been turning to the *Linux* Operating System, which is now the main competitor to Microsoft on PC computers. Linux advocates are impressed with its stability and security, generally reporting fewer problems with the computer "crashing" (when it has to be reset or powered off before working again) and fewer infections with malicious software agents such as computer viruses (more about that subject later). However, Linux has some limitations in the range of applications software it supports. Furthermore, it is not generally available pre-installed, and operating system installation is certainly not a task for a novice computer user! So all in all, Microsoft Windows is probably the best choice for general use on a home computer.

To summarise then, our suggested Net computer has a minimum configuration something like the following:

- **CPU:** Pentium III, 600MHz or equivalent.

- **RAM:** 64 MByte

- **Hard Disk:** 4 GByte

- **Floppy Disk:** 1.44 MByte

- **Video:** 1 MByte Video RAM, 800x600 resolution, 16-bit colour.

- **Modem:** 56 kbps/V90.

- **CD-ROM:** x12

- **Sound Support**

- **Operating System (PC):** Microsoft Windows.

As these are just minimum specifications you should feel free to exceed any or all of them if your budget runs to it.

Welcome Aboard

What Is This Internet Thing Anyway

Your Net Computer

Getting On-line

The Web

E-mail

Other Internet Services

Welcome Aboard

What Is This Internet Thing Anyway

Your Net Computer

Getting On-line

The Web

E-mail

Other Internet Services

All right, now that we know what the components are, and have at least a minimum specification in mind, let's briefly talk about buying a Net computer - or upgrading a computer you already have for Net use.

Buying A New Computer

If you do not already have a computer, you will need to buy one to use for Net access. This is a substantial investment - budget at least €1,000 - 1,500. So don't rush into anything. I have given a basic introduction to the various parts and what they are about, but you should certainly take time to investigate models from different shops and dealers before committing yourself to a purchase. If it is at all possible, you should find a friend or colleague who already owns a computer who will come along and advise you.

Perhaps the most important thing to remember is this: *When you are in a computer shop, you are the customer - so ask questions!* The *job* of the people working in the shop is to explain what they are trying to sell. And to keep on explaining - or demonstrating - until you understand. Don't be fobbed off with big words and technicalities: explaining the features of a computer should be no more complicated than for a washing machine or a VCR.

Ask, in particular, for demonstrations of the computer actually being used to access the Internet. Not only will you get a handy preview of what to expect on the Internet, but you can get a realistic comparison of how the different machines perform. Think of it like taking a car for a test drive: even after you've read all the brochures, and compared all the technical numbers and specifications, the real test is how it drives (or, in our case, "surfs"!).

Ask whether the machine comes with suitable Internet software already installed - and included in the price you are being quoted. Ask whether this is tailored for particular Internet Service Providers - companies that sell the Internet access service (we'll look at that issue in detail in the next chapter), and whether it's easy for you to select the provider of your own choice.

You may consider buying a new computer by telephone or mail order, or buying a second-hand computer through the classified advertisements. This *can* be a very good idea for people who know what they are doing - but you should examine the pros and cons carefully. If you are a complete beginner with computers, you may prefer to buy from a local, reputable shop or dealer - someone who is likely to still be around for the several years when you may need continuing advice, assistance, repairs and upgrades. You will pay a small premium for this, but may consider it worthwhile in the long run. If buying by telephone or mail order, again you should prefer the larger, established suppliers and take particular care to check the warranty agreement being offered.

Can't I Use The Computer I Already Have?

As everybody knows, computer technology is advancing at a furious rate. Somewhat strangely, computers don't actually seem to get much cheaper as a result. Instead they get more powerful, year by year, for much the same amount of cash. Unfortunately, the software to run on the computers also gets more sophisticated and demanding every year too: so if you want to be able to use the most recent facilities, you need to have a computer which is up to date. In fact, if you have a computer which is much more than two years old, it is already well behind the current state of the art. It *might* be possible to "upgrade" or add extra equipment to such a computer to make it suitable for satisfactory Internet access - but this upgrade may not be much cheaper than buying a whole new machine!

It is not feasible to cover the range of potential upgrade requirements here. If you are considering this possibility, then bring your machine along to a reputable computer supplier and ask their advice. Better yet, bring it to a few different suppliers and compare their advice! Again, if you can find a trusted friend or colleague to advise you, that is the best option of all. But one way or another, if you want to get the most out of the Internet, try to equip yourself with a computer with the minimum suggested specification given above.

Walk Before You Run!

OK, you have a PC. It's out of the box, all the parts have been connected together with all the right cables. You've carefully read the manuals that came with it, and checked and rechecked all the connections. You've switched on, it has hummed and warmed up, and the Windows *desktop* has appeared on your screen.

So are you ready to get on the Internet now? Well not quite. There is still a little homework to do - specifically to arrange for an Internet connection from an Internet Service Provider. I will cover that in the next chapter. But, if this is your first experience with a PC you will have to learn about its basic operation before worrying about the Internet connection. This book is about getting on the Internet, not about general use of a PC, so I can't cover the general skills of using a PC here. But I will leave you with a few quick beginners' hints:

- If you're buying a new computer from a computer shop or dealer, get them to walk you through all the setting up in the shop first. Ask for an explanation of exactly what Application Software is included. Get them to show you how to start up these programs. Get a demonstration of how to load CD-ROMs, and the operation of the printer. If possible, try connecting and starting up the computer yourself, in the shop, before you take it home.

Welcome Aboard

What Is This Internet Thing Anyway

Your Net Computer

Getting On-line

The Web

E-mail

Other Internet Services

Welcome Aboard

What Is This Internet Thing Anyway

Your Net Computer

Getting On-line

The Web

E-mail

Other Internet Services

- Work through the *Exploring Windows* programme. This is usually already installed, but if not, can be accessed on the Windows CD-ROM. If necessary, ask your supplier how to start it up. This provides an excellent introduction to the basic operation of your computer. It is very easy to follow and covers basic skills you'll use over and over again. It should take less than an hour to complete. Take this opportunity to familiarise yourself with the Windows *Help* system, which provides electronic documentation for your computer. Whenever you are learning to use a new Windows Application it will have additional electronic documentation which you can access through this system.

So now you've got your computer, and you have mastered its basic operations (even if the L-plates are still up). The next step is to decide what company is going to connect your computer to the Internet - your *Internet Service Provider.*

3. Getting Online: Choosing An Internet Service Provider (ISP)

T he Internet is a global network of computers. Simply speaking, these can be divided into clients and servers. Clients are computers like yours: they request services (information, e-mail, etc.) from other computers on the network. These other computers that *provide* services are called - surprise, surprise - *servers.*

Servers are generally powered up and connected to the Internet permanently. Clients may come and go all the time. Servers are operated by all kinds of organisations - companies, voluntary groups, state agencies and so on. They are there to provide access, through the Internet, to whatever services that organisation wants to offer.

In this chapter we are going to be concerned with one particular kind of server - and the companies which operate them. These are servers whose *essential* purpose in life is to connect clients to the rest of the Internet. They send information back and forth to other machines on the Internet on behalf of their particular clients. They are operated by companies whose business is precisely to sell the service of doing this - of connecting client machines to the Internet. They are the *Internet Service Providers,* or ISPs.

The idea is this: an ISP operates a number of server computers. These are operating continuously. They are connected together and to the rest of the Internet by permanent connections. These connections in turn are special high capacity data communication links (not normal phone lines) bought or leased by the ISP from a telecommunications company. So these servers belonging to the ISP are permanently able to forward or relay communications from their clients to the rest of the Net.

These ISP servers each have a number of modems connected to them. Remember modems? These are the devices which allow two computers to communicate over a conventional phone line. The ISP servers are continuously listening for incoming calls on these modems. When you want to have a session on the Net, your computer places a telephone call (via its modem) to the ISP, which gets routed automatically to the first available modem. It gets answered, and the two computers (your client and the ISP's server) go through some kind of negotiation to make sure you are authorised to connect. Then a connection is established and you are (finally!) "on" the Internet.

Welcome Aboard

What Is This Internet Thing Anyway

Your Net Computer

Getting On-line

The Web

E-mail

Other Internet Services

Welcome Aboard

What Is This Internet Thing Anyway

Your Net Computer

Getting On-line

The Web

E-mail

Other Internet Services

Whatever information you want to send or receive to or from *anywhere* on the Internet now gets routed via the ISP's server.

A Free Lunch, Anybody?

As everyone knows by now, access to the Internet in Ireland is free ... or is it? Actually, despite what you might have read or heard, there is still no such thing as a *completely* free lunch, and Internet access is no exception. However, there are now a variety of models for charging for Internet access, and it is important to have *some* understanding of how these operate.

To access the Internet you will *potentially* have to pay (at least) two different basic kinds of charge. Firstly, every time your computer makes a phone call to connect to the Internet, you are liable to be charged for that phone call in the normal way. The exact charge for each call may, in general, depend on a number of factors (the time of day, the duration of the call, the number you are calling from, your particular phone company, your particular ISP etc.). Secondly, you may pay an Internet "subscription fee"; this is typically charged per month or per year, and is independent of how often you connect, or how much or how little time you spend online. In general, call charges are levied by the phone company, who may, or may not, pass on some of this charge to your ISP, in the case of Internet calls; and subscription charges are levied by your ISP. Of course, in some cases, both your phone and Internet service may actually be delivered by the same company.

For a number of years the only model for Internet charging in Ireland was a *combination* of both call charges and subscription fees, albeit with some variation in the details. While combination schemes continue to be available - and are still suitable for many users - ISPs now generally also offer Internet service with *no* subscription fee, that is, funded exclusively from call charges. This is commonly referred to as "free" access; but clearly it is not really free, and is more properly called "pay-as-you-go." Another possibility, common in the US, is the very opposite service model, with no call charges, but rather funded exclusively from subscription fees. This is often called "flat-rate" access.

Finally, another major element in paying for Internet access is the availability of technical support for whenever you have problems. All ISP's generally offer such technical support. But while the details - and the charges! - vary significantly, it is worth noting that it is typical of the "free" (or pay-as-you-go) services that technical support is available *only* via a premium rate (i.e., quite expensive) phone call.

The Magic: Distance Independent Tariffs

However, despite the sometimes bewildering complexity of the different schemes of charging for Internet usage, there is still one piece of very good - and perhaps very surprising - news: the charges levied are completely independent of *how far around the world your data has to travel.* This means that you pay exactly the same whether you are sending e-mail to your brother in the next town, your uncle in England, or your ex-boyfriend in Australia. And you pay exactly the same for accessing a Web site in Dublin, Hong Kong or Rio de Janeiro. *The distance is absolutely irrelevant to the charge you pay.* This makes the Internet completely different in nature from previous communication technologies - telephone, fax, even the postal service. It is global in a genuine way that has never existed before.

Many people find this utterly crazy the first time they hear it. "Surely", they say "it must cost an Irish ISP more to communicate with Los Angeles than Letterkenny? So surely they have to charge me more accordingly?"

But that, precisely and unexpectedly, is what is *not* the case!

A combination of historical and technical factors is responsible for this strange situation. Very crudely, the extra cost involved in metering exactly where any given client's information comes from or goes to on the Internet would far outweigh the benefit of having more "accurate" billing. So all clients get billed according to the same "averaged" costs of the service - whether you happen to use it mostly for reading *The Irish Times* or *The New York Times*!

Are All ISPs Equal?

Internet service provision is somewhat of a "commodity" product. Like potatoes, pork bellies, or petrol, you can get *more or less* the same product from a number of different and competing suppliers. This is very good! The competition drives prices down, and ensures that the different suppliers have to stay efficient to stay competitive.

So does that mean that all ISPs are equal? Well, not quite.

Although the basic service - Internet access - is the same for all ISPs, the details can vary significantly from one to another. The ISP business is very dynamic with new companies entering and leaving the market all the time, not to mention the existing companies continuously offering new or different access service products. Which company, or even which particular access service, will suit you best will depend on your particular needs.

Welcome Aboard

What Is This Internet Thing Anyway

Your Net Computer

Getting On-line

The Web

E-mail

Other Internet Services

Welcome Aboard

What Is This Internet Thing Anyway

Your Net Computer

Getting On-line

The Web

E-mail

Other Internet Services

In this section I'll review some of the major factors to be considered in choosing an ISP. Note that the free CD-ROM accompanying this book provides software and instructions for Internet connection via *IOL*, one of Ireland's premier ISP companies, including a choice of both *free access* (pay-as-you-go) and *premium* (combined subscription/call charge) services. *IOL* are also exclusive sponsors of the book, and I'll be using the *IOL* services to illustrate the various issues raised here.

- ISPs do, of course, compete on *price* - but, as already explained, this is a very complex issue to evaluate, depending as it does on a wide variety of factors. I consider just a few of the more important of these here.

- A first price factor is the ISPs' network of Points of Presence or POPs. This is another piece of fairly unnecessary Internet technospeak. A POP is simply a location, or phone number, where the ISP offers dial-up connections. To minimise your call charges for Internet access, you want an ISP which you can connect to at local call rates - or lower. The *IOL Free* service offers local call access throughout the country; while the *IOL Gold* service offers access at specially reduced rate call charges, significantly lower even than normal local calls.

- Then there is the question of what kind of technical support service does the ISP provide? For example, is there a telephone helpline? What are its hours of operation? And most importantly, how much do calls cost? These are all especially important questions for new users. The *IOL* support desk operates from 9am to 10pm Monday to Friday, and 9am to 6pm on weekends (10am to 7pm on public holidays). If you avail of the *IOL Free* access service, then support calls are charged at a premium rate; but if you use the *IOL Gold* service then support calls are available at just local call rates throughout the country.

- Overall, competition tends to ensures that there are not dramatic price differentials between different ISPs, so the more significant issue here tends to be choice of a particular charging model. In general, if you have moderate usage, mainly in evenings or weekends, and do not require too much technical support, the *IOL Free* access service should be quite cost effective. However, if you require ongoing daytime usage, or if you need significant technical support, the *IOL Gold* service may well be better value.

- Another important factor is choosing an ISP is the *quality of service* they can offer. This relates to things like how often you get an engaged tone when trying to connect; or how quickly email is transferred between your computer and the ISP's mail server; or, more generally, how quickly your ISP can transfer data between your computer and the wider Internet. Roughly speaking, quality of service will reflect how much infrastructure the ISP has put in place *compared* to the number of clients it is trying to support. Unfortunately, there are currently no simple, independently assessed and published, measures of ISP quality of service. However, the availability of free access services now makes it much easier to sample different ISP's in order to form your own judgement on this.

- Check how *many* e-mail addresses an ISP will provide to you. Families, in particular, often find that it is convenient if each member can have his or her own separate e-mail address. All **IOL** services include the use of an unlimited number of email addresses.

- Does an ISP provide you with "web space", and if so, how much? Providing "web space" means that the ISP allows you to load information onto one of its computers which will then be available to anyone else in the world, at any time - regardless of whether your own computer is connected or not. In this way, you can publish your own information to a global audience, on any subject you like. (Of course, this doesn't in itself guarantee that anyone will actually want to read or download it...) This may seem a ridiculously remote possibility to you right now, before you have even connected to the Internet for the first time, but you may be surprised at how quickly you'll want to publish on the Net yourself! In any case, it is certainly worth checking that it is supported by any prospective ISP. The **IOL Free** access service provides for 10MByte of web space, which is ample for a small personal site; while the **IOL Gold** service includes 100MByte, sufficient even for a substantial business site.

So Now What?

The details of installing software and establishing your initial connection to the Internet will vary significantly from one ISP to another, so I will not attempt to go into them in detail here. If you still have that friend with an Internet account, who helped you buy or upgrade your PC, now would be a great time to invite him around! In any case, if you run into problems - and many people do - then just contact your ISP's technical support line. Then, once you have got a working connection to the Internet, you'll be ready to read on to the wonders of the World Wide Web!

Welcome Aboard

What Is This Internet Thing Anyway

Your Net Computer

Getting On-line

The Web

E-mail

Other Internet Services

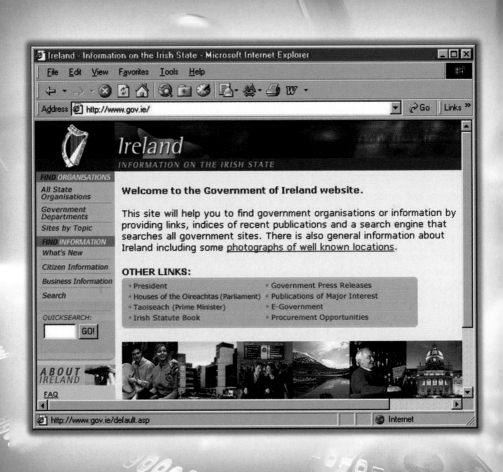

Ireland - Information on the Irish State - Microsoft Internet Explorer

File   Edit   View   Favorites   Tools   Help

Address 🔲 http://www.gov.ie/   ▼   🔗 Go   Links »

Ireland
INFORMATION ON THE IRISH STATE

FIND ORGANISATIONS
All State Organisations
Government Departments
Sites by Topic

FIND INFORMATION
What's New
Citizen Information
Business Information
Search

QUICKSEARCH:
[   ] GO!

ABOUT IRELAND
FAQ

Welcome to the Government of Ireland website.

This site will help you to find government organisations or information by providing links, indices of recent publications and a search engine that searches all government sites. There is also general information about Ireland including some <u>photographs of well known locations</u>.

OTHER LINKS:

• President
• Houses of the Oireachtas (Parliament)
• Taoiseach (Prime Minister)
• Irish Statute Book

• Government Press Releases
• Publications of Major Interest
• E-Government
• Procurement Opportunities

🔲 http://www.gov.ie/default.asp   🌐 Internet

4. The Web: An Ocean of Information

The great thing about the *World Wide Web* is that, beneath all the hype and hoopla there is a very simple idea at work - an idea called *hypertext*.

Now we all know what written *text* is: letters, numbers, punctuation marks and so on. These are strung together in a particular order to produce words, sentences, paragraphs, chapters and even whole books - just like the one you are holding in your hands. But stop for a moment, and take another look at that phrase "in a particular order".

When we read a book we usually start at the beginning, work our way through the middle and end up at the end. It's as if there is a straight line through the book, showing the order. This is called "linear text" to indicate the idea of an implied "line" or order to read it in. This is so obvious and so essential to the whole idea of a book or an article that we usually don't even refer to it explicitly at all. But not all texts are like this.

To see the need for "non-linear" texts, think about using a reference book such as an encyclopedia or a telephone directory. It would be very tedious - to say the least - to have to start at the start of the phone directory and work "linearly" through it, in order to find the number of your friend Ziggy Zoziemus. Or to find the encyclopedia article on *xylophones*. So, of course, you don't do that: instead, you *jump* into the book at (more or less) the correct point.

With the phone book this relies mainly on simple alphabetic ordering. With the encyclopedia it is made easier by providing an index. Once you find *xylophone* in the index, there is a reference (a page number) that allows you go *directly* to the article. That article may then direct you to other related articles - perhaps to the composer, Igor Stravinsky, who introduced a xylophone into his ballet *Petrushka* in 1912 (yes, I just looked it up in my encyclopedia). This cross-reference can also have a page number, so that you can immediately jump to that article. That one in turn can be linked to others (Diaghilev, Jazz, 20th century music...) and so on.

For a large encyclopedia things get more complicated. You may need a volume number as well as a page number to locate an article. Then perhaps there will be references to further readings which are not contained within the encyclopedia itself - other books, sheet music, recordings, videos, pamphlets and so on. We are now talking about something like the card catalogue in a library. Once you find the right card, it

Welcome Aboard

What Is This Internet Thing Anyway

Your Net Computer

Getting On-line

The Web

E-mail

Other Internet Services

Welcome Aboard

What Is This Internet Thing Anyway

Your Net Computer

Getting On-line

The Web

E-mail

Other Internet Services

effectively gives you directions on where to go in the library to find the particular book. Then, if you know the page number you want, you can jump right in.

You should be getting the idea that a lot of information in the world can be accessed in a variety of alternative orderings. You don't always have to follow the "obvious" ordering of the way the pages happen to be glued together to make a book, or the way the books are ordered on a library shelf. This idea of a text with many different entry points and many different pathways through it, is called a *hypertext*. The "hyper" is just a fancy label to distinguish it from a "linear" text. There is nothing complex or mysterious about it. The chances are, you have been happily using hypertexts all your life. It's just that nobody bothered to dress them up in this obscure jargon before now.

Hypermedia is just a small further extension of the hypertext idea. Here the blocks or pieces of information need not be limited to just textual materials, but can include other types of information, such as pictures, audio, animations and even video clips. The whole collection just has to offer multiple alternative pathways through it, by following "hyperlinks" - references from one arbitrary position to another - for it to be called "hypermedia".

So: hypertext and hypermedia are nothing new, and are not somehow unique inventions of the computer age. Your local library, with its books, photographs, paintings, audio and video tapes - and card catalogues providing connections between them - is one big hypermedia collection.

All the same, the computer age has made a big difference. Think again about using "hyperlinks" - cross references - within a conventional book. Certainly, it is a lot faster to jump to a page number than to have to read from the start to the point you want, but it can still be awkward. It is tolerable enough to follow links within one volume. It becomes a lot slower to follow links between volumes in, say, a 20-volume encyclopedia. And to follow a link from an encyclopedia to, say, a painting in an art gallery may involve a trip of thousands of miles, and take months or years in the planning and execution.

Electronic, computer-networked, hypermedia (phew!) change all that. First of all, hyperlinks within the "same" work can be followed instantaneously - no searching for the correct volume, no tedious flicking through to the correct page etc. Just use your mouse to point at the hyperlink or cross-reference, click on it, and presto, you're there. Better yet, a computer is just as happy to display sounds, pictures and videos as to display plain text. So you can follow a hyperlink directly to any of these kinds of information just as easily - you don't have to start up an entirely different machine to, say, listen to music.

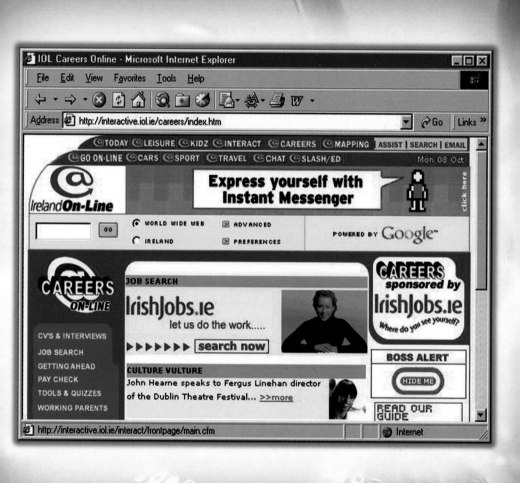

Welcome Aboard

What Is This Internet Thing Anyway

Your Net Computer

Getting On-line

The Web

E-mail

Other Internet Services

Now imagine that all of the information you might want to refer to is already available in electronic form, on *some* computer somewhere in the world. Imagine that all these computers are connected together by a network. Imagine that there is a standard way of describing exactly where each piece of information is located - such as the shelf-marks in the library, combined (if necessary) with the volume and page numbers. Imagine that this works to exactly locate *any* kind of information, on *any* computer, *anywhere* in the world. Using *these* globally standardised references, you can follow hyperlinks between completely different sources of information, located in completely different parts of world, just as easily as you can follow links within a single book or document. Better yet, your computer can do it for you: just click on the hyperlink and your computer will contact the right server, and download the information you want. No matter where in the world it is, you could view it right from your own desk.

Imagine all of that, and you have imagined the *World Wide Web!* Well, that's the big idea. Now I need to get down to specifics.

The Web Browser: Your Global Library Card

The software you use to access the Web is called a *browser* - because you can use it to browse through any of the information provided on the Web, anywhere in the world. If you bought a new computer recently there may well be a browser already installed. If not, your ISP should have provided you with a browser program in the software startup kit. The two most popular browsers are *Netscape Navigator* (part of the *Communicator* suite) and *Microsoft Internet Explorer*. These are very similar to each other both in concept and function. The *IOL* software kit on the CD-ROM accompanying the book includes Internet Explorer, which I will accordingly use for illustration in this chapter. Note that this discussion may not match what you see on your own system exactly - as with most software packages, Internet Explorer is updated and enhanced on an ongoing basis, which may therefore give rise to some detailed discrepancies.

A Session On The Web

So what is this mysterious activity called *surfing the Web?* The Web is a network of "units" of information. I'll refer to a single "unit" as an information *resource*. Information resources are of various types and kinds.

The single most common kind of resource is like a page in a book or magazine - mainly textual, but potentially incorporating photographs, diagrams or other graphics and illustrations. Resources like that are usually formated in what is technically called *HyperText Markup Language,* or HTML. We will often refer to an HTML resource as a Web *page,* but be warned that this can be a little misleading. For example, if you print out one of these "pages" it may well require 5, 10 or even more pages of printing.

Other kinds of resources might be audio or video clips, animations or even pages that allow some form of *interaction* with a remote server computer, such as getting a price quotation or placing an order. Now we can say just what it means to "Surf the Web":

- You first access an information resource. That is to say, your browser retrieves or "downloads" the resource from the server computer that holds it. Then the browser displays the resource for you. Of course, the exact meaning of "display" depends on the particular type of resource. In any case, many resources will have further links embedded within them. These are connections or pointers to other resources. The browser will use some distinctive mechanism to indicate the presence of these links. Each link will usually give a brief description or explanation of the other resource it is pointing at.

- So, once you have viewed (read, played, listened to, whatever) the resource, you decide what other related resources you want to access - which is to say, what link you want to follow. Then you *select* the link, and that new resource will be retrieved. And so on.

That's it - that's all that this obscure and weird sounding "surfing" is about. You can compare it to wandering around - browsing! - in a bookshop or library. You read something at one location. That refers to something elsewhere, so you go and have a look at that. It then refers to something else, and so on.

There are a few variations on this simple scheme, of course. You may follow a link, but then decide it wasn't really interesting, so you retrace your steps back to an earlier point. You may get bored with a particular subject, and decide to jump to some completely other information resource, without following any link at all. You may want to use some kind of more systematic approach than this rather random sounding "browsing". There are tools - so-called *search engines* - which try to identify all in one go the resources that might be of interest to you.

But the basic model of using the Web is still just what I have described here: you access or download a resource; you examine it and you then select another one. That really is all there is to it! However, notice how very different this is to the broadcast media - radio and television. Or even to most print media, such as newspapers. You just can't be a couch potato on the Web (what a vision!). You can't sit back and wait for someone else to decide what information to beam at you, in what order. You must constantly decide for yourself where to go next, what to look up, what links to follow. It takes a little while getting used to, but then it is a really heady experience. Dizzying even. Perhaps *surfing* is a pretty good description after all!

Welcome Aboard

What Is This Internet Thing Anyway

Your Net Computer

Getting On-line

The Web

E-mail

Other Internet Services

Welcome Aboard

What Is This Internet Thing Anyway

Your Net Computer

Getting On-line

The Web

E-mail

Other Internet Services

So What's A Web Site?

As I have described so far, there is only one "level" of organisation on the Web - the single information resource or Web page that you can access at a time. In practice, the Web is a little bit more organised than that (though not much!). Much of the available information is structured into collections of resources that are more or less closely related to each other. Such a collection is called a single Web *site*.

A Web site is often associated with a single organisation. So we refer to the *Microsoft* site, or *The Irish Times* site, or the *Amnesty International* site. But there are also sites devoted to particular subjects, for example, sites for individual people (Galileo, Karl Popper, Madonna), or sites for events (The FA Premiership, The World Chess Championship). A site often corresponds to all the information on a single web server computer - but not always: a single server may host information divided into a number of different sites.

In any case, while it's handy to have an idea what people mean when they refer to a web "site", it is not a very hard or fast category. By the very nature of the Web, there will be links not just between the resources making up one site, but also to resources in other, separate sites. So, in a sense, calling a particular collection a single site is always going to be somewhat in the eye of the beholder.

What's Another URL?

Each resource on the Web can contain hyperlinks to other resources. It is precisely this network of connections that *constitutes* the "web". So a single hyperlink *uniquely* and *exactly* identifies how and where to find one information resource. In order to do this there must be a completely standardised format for expressing the "address" of each information resource. This format is the basis for *Uniform Resource Locators* or URLs.

Here is a simple example of a URL, which can be broken into a number of separate parts:

```
http://www.amnesty.ie/about/udhr.shtml
```

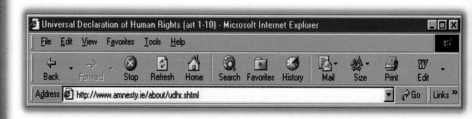

- First we have the "protocol" part, which is whatever comes before the ":" character. In my example, it is `http`. The protocol explains how your computer must "talk" to the remote computer to retrieve this particular information resource. Just in the same way that people need to speak the same language in order to have a meaningful conversation, so computers need to follow the same "protocol" if they are to exchange information. `http` stands for HyperText Transfer Protocol. It's the single most common protocol for accessing information on the Web, but there are a number of others, such as `ftp`, `gopher` and `https`. Fortunately, you need not worry about the details of what exactly these protocol codes stand for. The point is that the computers will choose the right way of talking to each other, and they will do this automatically, based on the protocol component of the URL. In fact, you can often omit the protocol part altogether, and the computers will still successfully identify the correct one to use.

- The next part of the URL is the *server name*. That is the name of the server computer that the information resource is located on. Every server in the world has a unique name.

  The server name consists of a small number of components connected by dots - usually three or four, but sometimes more. In my example, it is `www.amnesty.ie`. This can be read a bit like a postal address: it identifies one particular computer, called `www`, within an organisation identified as `amnesty`, and geographically located in Ireland (`.ie`). Let's look at each compnent in turn in a little more detail, working from the right (the most general) to the left (the most specific).

  The last component of the server name is often a two-letter code identifying a country: `.ie` for Ireland, `.uk` for the United Kingdom, `.br` for Brazil and so on. Alternatively it can be a non-geographical code, such as `.com` for a commercial organisation, `.edu` for an educational institution, or the general purpose `.net,` etc. Sites using these non-geographical codes may be located anywhere in the world.

  The second last component of the server name usually indicates an organisation of some sort, perhaps a company, or a state agency, or an educational institution. In our case, `amnesty` stands for the human rights organisation, *Amnesty International*. Many organisations embed their names in server names in this way, for example, `www.gov.ie` identifies the Irish Government web server, and `www.dcu.ie` identifies that of DCU (Dublin City University).

Welcome Aboard

What Is This Internet Thing Anyway

Your Net Computer

Getting On-line

The Web

E-mail

Other Internet Services

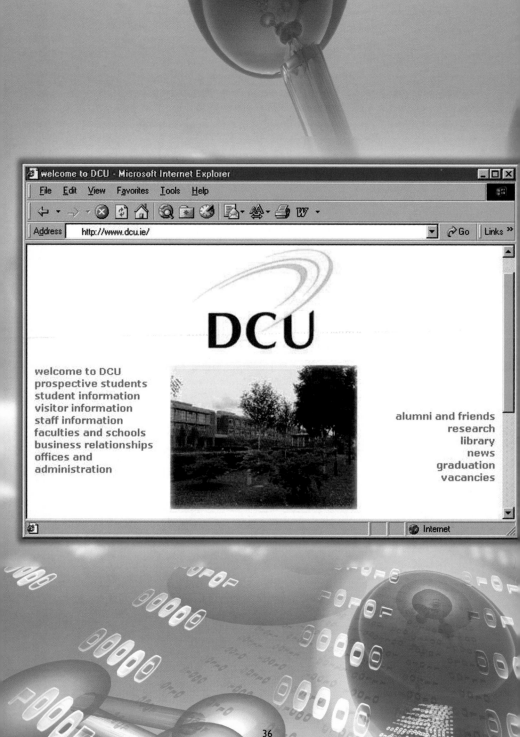

There may be other "middle" components of the server name. If so, they tend to indicate a section or department within an organisation. For example, `www.eeng.dcu.ie` identifies a server in the Electronic Engineering Department (`eeng`) of Dublin City University (`dcu`).

The first component of the server name is used to uniquely identify a particular server within an organisation. This can be needed because any given organisation, or even department within an organisation, may operate a number of different servers. It is very common for the server which provides access to an organisation's primary public World Wide Web site to be called `www`. As a result, server names in URLs often start with `www`. But they don't have to, and you will often see variations on this, such as `sport.iol.ie` for example, which identifies a separate *IOL* server which hosts sports related stories and resources.

- The remainder of the URL, following the server name, identifies a particular *file*, or information resource, on the server computer. Information on a computer is often organised like a filing cabinet, with files within folders, and folders within a cabinet (server). So in my example, `about` identifies a particular folder (containing general information "about" Amnesty International), and `udhr.shtml` names one particular file within that folder (an electronic copy of the UN *Universal Declaration of Human Rights*). The `.shtml` code at the end of the file name is a hint that this file contains information formatted in some form or variant of HTML. Again, we will not worry about these details: the browser will automatically talk to the server to find out exactly what the format of the resource is, and how it should be displayed.

Generally you need not be concerned about the exact format of URLs when you use the Web. The whole point of having standardised addresses is that it allows a browser to automatically follow them. In fact, a lot of the time, you need not even know the URL for an information resource - you just click on a hyperlink and the resource appears.

But explicit URLs are *sometimes* useful. In particular, if you come across an interesting resource on the Web, and you want to tell other people about it, it is useful to know that all you need send them is a copy of the URL. Once they have that unique, global, address, they will be able to access that same resource themselves. That is why you now see URLs incorporated in advertising materials, business cards, and letter heads: once you have the URL you can follow up to locate a whole range of linked materials.

URLs look very complex at first, but if you can remember that they are just glorified page numbers you will soon get used to them.

Welcome Aboard

What Is This Internet Thing Anyway

Your Net Computer

Getting On-line

The Web

E-mail

Other Internet Services

Welcome Aboard

What Is This Internet Thing Anyway

Your Net Computer

Getting On-line

The Web

E-mail

Other Internet Services

Ladies And Gentlemen: Start Your Browsers!

As already mentioned, I will be using Microsoft Internet Explorer, or simply MS-IE, operating under the Microsoft Windows Operating System, as my example browser. Other browsers and Operating Systems will be similar in concept.

I will assume that your computer is switched on and waiting for you, that you have already completed the installation of the software kit from your ISP, and that you have established that you can successfully connect to the ISP. Many aspects of operating or interacting with programs on an MS-Windows computer are very standardised. So if you are already familiar with other applications - such as word processing, using a spreadsheet and so on - then you will find that experience very useful in getting started with MS-IE. I will assume that you are familiar with basic operations such as using the mouse, starting applications, moving and resizing windows on the screen, and using scroll bars. So: start up MS-IE now, by double clicking on its icon on your computer desktop.

Unless your computer has already, for some reason, dialed up your ISP and established your connection to the Internet, this will now happen automatically as you start up MS-IE. You should already have gone through this process at the end of installing the software kit from your ISP. If you run into problems now, you will need to contact the ISP technical support desk. For our purposes, I will assume the connection works, and that MS-IE is running successfully.

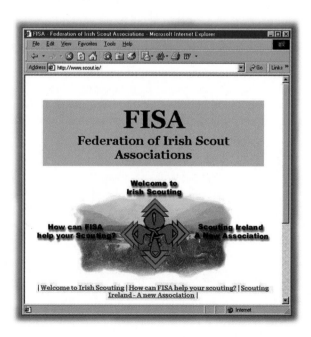

Anatomy Of A Browser

MS-IE initially displays a single large window on screen. The top of the window carries a *Title Bar*. This will normally display a short title for whatever information resource or page is currently being viewed. The Title Bar also supports a variety of standard MS-Windows operations such as moving the window around, resizing it, and closing the application down. Again, we'll assume here that you have already mastered these. Below the Title Bar is the *Menu Bar*. When you click on one of the words on the Menu Bar a menu of possible actions will drop down.

Below the Menu Bar is the *Tool Bar*. This is a collection of buttons with little icons that give quick access to certain operations that are used frequently. MS-IE also has a special "Activity" icon at the extreme right of the Tool Bar. This will be animated during downloads to indicate the ongoing activity. Underneath the Tool Bar are the *Address Bar,* the *Go Button*, and the *Links Bar*. The Address Bar shows the address (URL) of whatever resource is being displayed or accessed. The Go Button is used to "go to" (access) a URL which has been manually entered in the Address Bar. The Links Bar provides a set of pre-configured links to particular resources on the Web.

Now we come to the main part or "pane" of the MS-IE window. This is the viewing area, used to display HTML Web pages when they are downloaded. Finally, at the bottom of the Window is a Status Bar. This is used to display the status, or progress, of MS-IE as it is downloading a resource.

Follow The Yellow Brick HyperLink...

Now we're ready to discuss the mechanics of browsing or "surfing". Your browser is probably configured to automatically load a page from your ISP's Web site when it starts up, such as `http://www.iol.ie/` (the *IOL portal* - I will explain this idea of a portal in more detail later). This may take a few seconds after the connection is made, but you should see it progressively loading as different parts are retrieved. You'll also see the Activity Icon animated during this process. Note that you will often have to use the *scroll bars* at the bottom or right of the main window pane to view the whole page. You will also usually find it helpful to *maximise* the MS-IE window while browsing the Web.

This initial page will typically be a mixture of text and graphics. Read through your initial page now. Try to pick out the *hyperlinks*. These will be pieces of text highlighted in some way, presented in a distinctive colour, often underlined as well. Buttons, icons, or other graphic images in the page may also be *hyperlinks*. In any case, you can easily check if something is a hyperlink by moving the mouse pointer onto it. If it is a link, a message will appear in the Status Bar giving some kind of indication of what it is a link to. (Note that Microsoft also sometimes use the term "shortcut" to mean hyperlink.)

Welcome Aboard

What Is This Internet Thing Anyway

Your Net Computer

Getting On-line

The Web

E-mail

Other Internet Services

Welcome Aboard

What Is This Internet Thing Anyway

Your Net Computer

Getting On-line

The Web

E-mail

Other Internet Services

Now pick a link and follow it: just move the mouse pointer over it and click. MS-IE will immediately attempt to retrieve that new resource. The Activity Icon will be animated, and the Status Bar will give a running indication of progress. As pieces of the new resource are retrieved they will appear in the main display pane.

Try this a few times, following some links from one page to another. Keep your balance because - congratulations! - you are now officially *Surfing*.

From Browsing To Navigating

OK, once the euphoria has died down, what next?

Well you now know how to go "forward" - just click on a link and you go to another resource. But each page will usually have a whole lot of *different* ways of going "forward", different places to go next. So, having followed one link forward, you will then often want to go "backward" to the previous page, so that you can explore one of the alternative links from there.

No problem. Remember the MS-IE *Tool Bar?* Well, take another look and you'll see two buttons labelled with arrows, one pointing left (**Back**) and the other pointing right (**Forward**). If you click on the **Back** button ⇐ you'll get back to the page you were previously looking at. If you've already followed several links forward, you can use **Back** repeatedly, and eventually get back to your initial start-up page. And once you have gone back you can go forward again. The **Forward** button ⇒ will bring you forward, automatically following the same links you followed the first time. If you want to go forward along a different route, you can diverge at any point simply by clicking on some new link rather than the **Forward** button.

Practise going forward and backward a few times. You will see how these buttons allow you to retrace a path that you've already taken from resource to resource, whereas clicking on a link starts a new diverging path. You are now not just Surfing but actually *Navigating* the Web - which sounds much more impressive!

Now let's look at the other buttons on the Tool Bar.

 Stop Button: If you have not already noticed it, some Web pages can take quite some time to download. Various factors affect this. The speed with which data can be moved down the phone line between you and your ISP is limited. There can be more or less severe bottlenecks at other points of the Internet route between you and a specific resource. The servers for particularly popular Web sites sometimes find it difficult to keep up with all the requests coming in. Pages with lots of fancy images or animations or sounds are also much slower to download that those with plain text. The nett effect is that you may find yourself twiddling your thumbs and regretting having tried to follow a particular link. That is when you reach for the **Stop Button**: this immediately stops the loading of whatever resource was being accessed.

Refresh: Clicking on this button causes the page you are already viewing to be reloaded. This might sound pretty pointless at first, but there are times when it is very useful. Many resources on the Web are dynamic - changing all the time. For example, a page might be showing current stock market prices or football scores. Then you might well want to reload it to get the more up-to-the-minute version. In the early days of the Web this was a very common situation, though it is becoming less so. Newer Web technologies actually make it possible for servers and browsers to automatically arrange for this updating as necessary, in which case, of course, you do not need to manually click the **Refresh** button. Still, it's handy to have, just in case.

 Home: The Web literally is *World Wide*. It is difficult to keep an accurate estimate of how many separate pages are available through it - indeed, there is some disagreement as to what exactly should count as "separate" anyway. But by any reasonable measure, there are now tens of millions of such distinct resources. Because of the nature of hypermedia, each of these can be linked to many others. Again it is difficult to give an exact figure, but the "typical" number of onward links is somewhere between ten and a hundred. Even taking ten as a conservative figure, this means that, from any given page, there are about a million other pages you can reach within only six mouse clicks.

The upshot of all this is that it is extremely easy to become totally lost in hyperspace. Once you have followed fifteen or twenty links (including backing up and going "forward" again a few times), you can become totally disoriented as to where you are, where you've come from, and even where - if anywhere - you are trying to get to.

This is where the **Home** button becomes useful. It simply returns you to whatever has been configured as your Home page. This is the same page at which your browser started - such as the *IOL* portal at `http://www.iol.ie/`. So it's a fixed point you always know you can easily return to if you get lost.

Having said that, the ability to jump back to a Home page is useful primarily to people just beginning to explore the Web. As you become more sophisticated, you will find that the *Favorites* mechanism (discussed later in this chapter) is a more powerful and general purpose tool than the simple **Home** button.

 Search: I have already explained that the Web is vast. Granted, it is also densely connected. There are many, many different ways or routes from any one page to another. You might think that, because of this rich network of connections, it should be easy to quickly find available resources on any subject you might be interested in, but unfortunately that is not the case.

Part of the reason for this is that a lot of the information resources on the Web are of very poor quality. By comparison with conventional, paper-based publications, it is extremely cheap to make information available via the Web. This encourages the

Welcome Aboard

What Is This Internet Thing Anyway

Your Net Computer

Getting On-line

The Web

E-mail

Other Internet Services

availability of some very poor materials indeed. Worse still, as yet there is no fully satisfactory or widely accepted mechanism for publishers to charge for access to resources on the Web. This means that there is limited incentive to design high quality resources for Web publication. I will return to this issue again at the end of the chapter.

There are also other deeper reasons why it can be extremely difficult to find useful information simply by browsing. Though you may be within a few links of a page you want, there will generally be vastly more pathways that fail to take you there than there are pathways that succeed.

So random surfing - which is what I have talked about so far - may be quite entertaining for a while, but for serious work you need more serious tools. You need something to help you quickly focus in on the part of the Web that is of interest.

The current answer to this is a so-called search engine. Roughly speaking, the idea is that you can hand a word, or a few words, or a few phrases, to a special "searching" program, running on a server computer on the Web. This server computer already has an index of all the words and all the phrases on all the pages anywhere on the Web. It looks up your words or phrases in its index, and then hands you back a list of the pages that match. This all happens within a few seconds. You can then follow these links directly to the pages that are likely to interest you, bypassing those that are not.

So, when you click on the MS-IE **Search** button, you will be presented with a separate pane in the MS-IE window which gives you access to a number of search engines. There will be a space for you to type in the words or phrases to search for, and a button you can click to commence the search. Alternatively, as you become more experienced, you can access the search engines of your choice directly (via "forms", accessed with a URL in the usual way). For example, the *IOL* portal provides direct access to the *Google* search engine including a unique Ireland only search - my own personal favourite.

The idea of a search engine sounds wonderful, but the reality is a little more complicated. First of all, there is the little matter of how to *create* an index of all the information on the Web. Not only is the Web vast, but it is dynamic, with new resources being added, and old ones being modified or removed, all the time. So no index of the Web is now, or ever will be, complete or accurate. This is why it is useful that there are multiple search engines, with different strengths and weaknesses.

There are two quite different strategies to indexing the Web. One can use an automated "robot" to go out, fetch resources, index them, follow links, index them, and so on. Or a person can manually look at pages and decide how to classify them, and order the index into meaningful categories. Both methods have their advantages and disadvantages. Automated indexing is relatively fast and cheap, but crude: these systems can only look at the raw words in a page, not the meaning behind them. The words you search on may also appear on many pages which have little good or useful information. Manual indexing is slow and expensive, so it can't be as complete or up to date, but it can be much more perceptive and accurate in the classification of the pages that *are* indexed.

In both cases, some care and skill may be required to phrase a search that will secure the results you want. For example, a search on the word "football" will certainly find pages on soccer, but also American football, rugby, and possibly Australian, Gaelic and maybe even a few others. Or a search on "computer games" will be pointless because it will find far too many pages matching this phrase - thousands, if not hundreds of thousands. Computer games are, not surprisingly, a very popular topic on the Web. Like anything else, you will find that you will get better with practice, especially as you get a feel for the distinct "personalities" of the different search engines.

The bottom line is that search engines are a powerful tool to help you navigate the Web. But you will still have to spend some time browsing and evaluating the sites thrown up by the search. It is probably best to think of the search engine as suggesting some possible starting points for further browsing. It is then up to you to sort the wheat from the chaff.

Favorites: Let us suppose that you have found a resource on the Web that you find really useful. You would like to be able to go back and visit it again in the future - perhaps because it gets updated over time, or it is a good starting point for further browsing. There is an obvious way of doing this. As I said at the start, any resource or page on the Web is uniquely identified by its URL. Whatever page you are currently visiting, its URL will be displayed somewhere by the browser. With MS-IE, it will appear in the Address Bar. So all you have to do is write

Welcome Aboard

What Is This Internet Thing Anyway

Your Net Computer

Getting On-line

The Web

E-mail

Other Internet Services

Welcome Aboard

What Is This Internet Thing Anyway

Your Net Computer

Getting On-line

The Web

E-mail

Other Internet Services

that URL down. Next time you want to visit, just type it in again. To do this with MS-IE, you can click in the Address Bar, delete the old URL (if any), type in the new URL, and click on the *Go* button to go there.

This is perfectly satisfactory for keeping track of a small number of short URLs. However, you will soon discover some disadvantages to this approach. As you accumulate a larger number of URLs you will find it hard to remember which was which. So you will find it helpful to attach some short, meaningful, text or title to each URL to remind you what it points to. You will come across some URLs which are rather long and complex - and thus error prone, both to write down in the first place, and to re-enter when you want to use them. These various factors will quickly combine to make you want some kind of more convenient, and automatic, mechanism for keeping track of favorite sites.

Fortunately, this is precisely the sort of dull, boring, and routine task that computers are really good at, and so we come to the **Favorites** button in MS-IE, or the **Bookmarks** button in Netscape Navigator, or some equivalent facility in other common browsers.

The basic idea is simply to allow the *computer* to record, sort, and keep track of your favourite URLs for you. It can automatically pick up a URL from the Address Bar, tag it with the title text attached to the page (if any) and store it away for future use. It can allow you to sort or organise these URLs, add additional explanatory notes, and, of course, return to any of these resources at any time. Best of all, it does all this quickly, accurately, and doesn't require you to keep track of little bits of paper! You can see now why I said that the **Home** button is just a special example of the facility provided by the **Favorites** button: it's just like programming a single button to point at your "mega-favourite" site.

I will not attempt to explain all the details of the Favorites facility here. Once you have the general idea of what the facility is about, then using it is generally fairly straightforward, and you can use the online help facility of MS-IE to get more details as necessary.

When MS-IE is first installed a number of Favorite sites are normally pre-configured for you. You will find this a useful set of initial suggestions for places you might like to visit. Of course, if you decide at any point that you are not interested in any of these sites, and prefer not to have them cluttering up your own set of favorites, then you can simply delete them.

 History: As well as allowing you to explicitly record sites you may wish to re-visit, via the Favorites facility, MS-IE also *automatically* records a "history" of sites you go to. So, if you want to check back on locations you have visited in previous days or even weeks, just click on the **History** button to access this record.

Mail: Clicking on the Mail button is simply a handy way of starting up your e-mail "client" program. This is configurable, but would typically give you access to Microsoft Outlook Express. Using e-mail will be the subject of the next chapter. You might wonder why the browser should be so tightly connected to an e-mail application. The historical reason is that Web pages often have e-mail addresses mentioned within them, so it can be very convenient to be able to easily switch from a browser to an e-mail program, typically by just clicking on a name or e-mail address. Since the browser needs to have this capability for starting an e-mail application anyway, it is easy to add a button to do the same thing.

 Size: This button gives you access to a menu of different font sizes for the text of the displayed Web page. A "font" means simply a particular style and size of character. MS-IE typically offers five distinct size settings. If you change the font setting, the change will be retained from one session to the next. The **Size** button has no effect on the size of *images* embedded in a page: they remain the same size, while the surrounding text changes.

The advantage of being able to adjust the font is that, depending on the size of your particular screen, and your eyesight, you may well find it more comfortable to view pages with larger or smaller sized fonts. This was considered a compelling attraction by the original designers of the HTML specification. However, there is also a disadvantage, in that the person designing the page cannot know in advance what font you will use, and therefore cannot know or control in advance exactly how the page will look. It follows that many pages do not look well in some font settings. This has been a source of much ongoing argument within the community of Web publishers. The HTML standard has now evolved to allow authors and designers to achieve much tighter control of how their material is presented - should they choose to exercise this control. In the future we will probably see an increasing trend toward tighter control of presentation. Correspondingly, the **Size** button may become less useful, or less disruptive, depending on your point of view.

 Print: This is pretty obvious: click this button to print the page you are currently viewing. Simple as it is, there are a few extra considerations to be aware of. Much of the material on the Web makes extensive use of colour: if you want to preserve this in printed versions, you will obviously need a colour printer! Conversely, even if you have a *colour* printer, you may not want to print in colour, for example, if you are only interested in reading the text, and therefore do not want to use up a lot of the colour cartridges in your printer. Unfortunately, the details of how to do this will vary from browser to browser and from printer to printer, so you will have to explore the online help for your particular set-up for more information.

Welcome Aboard

What Is This Internet Thing Anyway

Your Net Computer

Getting On-line

The Web

E-mail

Other Internet Services

Welcome Aboard

What Is This Internet Thing Anyway

Your Net Computer

Getting On-line

The Web

E-mail

Other Internet Services

Note again that what is called a "page" in Web terminology rarely corresponds directly to a physical page of paper when it is printed. You may also find that the exact layout of the material - positioning of graphics, line breaks in the text etc, may be different in the printed version compared to what you have seen on screen. This is quite normal.

Many beginners on the Web assume that printing Web material out is the only way to continue reading it after going offline (i.e., ending the Internet phone call). This is not so. Firstly, any page you are actually viewing will remain visible in the browser even when you hang up the phone connection, so you can then complete reading it at your leisure. Furthermore, if you don't actually want to complete reading it at that time, you can generally save an electronic copy of the page on your own computer, so that you can reload it again, even after shutting down and restarting the computer, and without having to make a fresh telephone connection to the Internet. The details of this will vary from browser to browser; in the case of recent versions of MS-IE you should consult the electronic documentation (via the `Help` menu) under the topic *Browsing the Web Offline*.

 Edit: This button will try to start up an appropriate application to allow you to *edit* the information you are viewing in MS-IE. Note carefully that this only means editing the local copy of the information which has been downloaded by MS-IE - it cannot generally allow you change the actual original information resource on the Web. Editing a Web resource is sometimes useful if you want to save and annotate your local copy. It can also be useful as a step toward publishing information on your own Web site (we'll return to that in the next section).

The Wide Blue Yonder...

In this chapter I have shown you the basics of using the Web. As you become more experienced you will quickly come across more advanced and exciting features. I cannot cover all these here, but I can at least whet your appetite.

I have concentrated on basic HTML resources, static pages with text and graphics. These are still the staple of the Web, but they are increasingly being complemented with other formats and types of media.

Even for basic text and graphics, HTML is not always the ideal choice. I have already mentioned that HTML only gives limited control of presentation to the document author or publisher. This can result in the same document appearing very differently to different users, depending on how they have configured their browsers. Often, the resulting visual presentation is not what the author intended, and is less than ideal.

There is a further complication when the same information is being made available in both electronic and paper forms. It is then often very important to have details of appearance (such as page numbers) match up exactly in both forms. An alternative to HTML which overcomes these problems is the *Portable Document Format*, or PDF, developed by Adobe Inc. The appearance of PDF documents is completely and precisely controlled by the author, and will appear exactly the same - as far as possible - on every computer or printed hardcopy. For this reason, it tends to be preferred over HTML, at least by "traditional" professional graphic designers. While PDF seems unlikely to challenge HTML as the mainstream format for textual document publication on the Web, it will probably maintain a significant minority role whenever the detailed layout and appearance of the document are critical.

Going beyond text, an obvious enhancement is provision of audio and video materials. Originally these were provided in "batch" or "non-streaming" formats. This meant that a complete sound or video clip had to be received before any of it could be played. This introduced a significant initial delay which made viewing of audio and video very frustrating and unsatisfactory. However, *streaming* audio and video are now becoming available. "Streaming" means that the information is "played" at the same time as it is being received. Streaming also allows live events or performances to be relayed. The quality of this media is still generally quite inferior to broadcast TV or radio, but this is offset by the very significant advantage of being able to access the materials you want "on demand". For example, RTE maintains an archive of selected daily and weekly radio programmes at:

`http://www.rte.ie/radio/av.html`

If it is not already installed on your computer, you will need the special **RealPlayer** software in order to playback these materials; but a basic version is available for free download - details are available from the RTE site above. I find this site very convenient as I can listen to programmes whenever it suits me, rather than when they happen to be broadcast. It is likely that, as this technology improves further, we will see more and more audio and video materials being made available on the Web.

Another growing feature of the Web is the provision of *interactive* services. Instead of simply downloading "static" information, interactive Web resources allow you to control or interact with your own computer, with server computers, and even with other people on the Web, in a unique and personalised way. This is an area which has attracted more than its fair share of new jargon (*Java, Weblets,* "active content" and many more). Don't be put off by this: the technological details don't matter to you as an end user. All that matters is that lots of new and imaginative interactive functionality is becoming available, opening up all kinds of opportunities for new services to be offered via the Web. These include home banking, shopping, playing games (everything from the traditional, such as chess and bridge, to the latest shoot-

Welcome Aboard

What Is This Internet Thing Anyway

Your Net Computer

Getting On-line

The Web

E-mail

Other Internet Services

Welcome Aboard

What Is This Internet Thing Anyway

Your Net Computer

Getting On-line

The Web

E-mail

Other Internet Services

em-up video games), personalised news bulletins, investment portfolios etc. Indeed, as mentioned in chapter 2, video game consoles are now beginning to offer Internet access built-in, specifically to support users across the globe being able to compete directly against each other. The potential is enormous and we can expect to see many, and more imaginative, interactive Internet services in the future.

Another related development is the emergence of *server push* technology. Yet again, this is a complicated term hiding a simple idea. As I have described the Web so far, I have focused almost entirely on you, the user, requesting or "pulling" information from the Web. Server "push" technology simply means that you can arrange for information to be automatically and routinely delivered to you on an ongoing basis - you do not have to repeatedly request updates. Server push essentially adds a mechanism for old fashioned *broadcasting* to the Web, and the terminology reflects this: the providers of these services offer "channels" of information which you "tune in to". The obvious applications are for information sources that are continuously changing - news, weather reports, sports results, stock market prices and so on. There is certainly a useful niche for this kind of application on the Web.

As already mentions in the case of audio and video materials, these various, more advanced, Web facilities may require some special software to support them. Generally this comes in the form of browser *plug-ins* - meaning no more and no less than that the extra software is closely integrated with a particular browser - and may not be supported by all browsers. Some plug-ins are usually included along with the browser itself, and will be automatically installed. In any case, if you attempt to access a new type of resource for which you do not already have a suitable plug-in, you should be warned of this, and usually prompted with where (on the Web itself!) to fetch the plug-in from, and how to install it. Basic plug-ins are usually free, though more sophisticated versions, with extra features, may be offered at some added cost.

And Now For The Bad News...

The first bad news - which you will figure out for yourself pretty quickly - is that although the Web is high tech, it can also *sometimes* be painfully slow and unreliable. This is partly a result of history: the technology underlying the Internet in general was never designed to be used on its current huge scale. It is also a result of the Web's explosive success. Every day the demands being made on the Internet are expanding rapidly - primarily as a result of increased Web-related traffic. The capacity of the Internet is expanding, but it is difficult for this expansion to keep up with demand, not least because there is no single central owner or manager of the Internet to co-ordinate this growth. Although the Internet was designed to be very robust, it achieves this robustness at a cost: whenever demand transiently exceeds capacity on some part of the Internet, that traffic begins to slow down. Sometimes it slows down a *lot* in the Internet equivalent of *gridlock*.

Welcome Aboard

What Is This Internet Thing Anyway

Your Net Computer

Getting On-line

The Web

E-mail

Other Internet Services

There is also a particular reliability problem introduced by the very rapid growth of the Internet. This affects the ability of the Internet to keep track of the relationship between the names of computers on the Internet and their underlying "IP numbers". The IP numbers are what actually control the routing of data through the network. Because so many new machines are being added, and so many requests are being generated for translations between names and numbers, the system for doing this translation (the Domain Name System or DNS) can get temporarily overloaded. This can give rise to very peculiar things. Suddenly you may be told that a site on the Web, which you had no difficulty accessing half an hour ago, now simply "does not exist" or "cannot be found".

Quite aside from the capacity limits of the core Internet network, individual server computers that make up the Web may become heavily overloaded. This can also manifest itself in severely slowed down communication, or in a temporary inability to access certain sites.

And all of this is quite aside from normal breakdowns and routine maintenance. In a network the size of the Internet, there are bound to be parts of it that are out of action for one reason or another, all the time.

The only point of this is to warn you to *expect* some significant degree of unreliability. During most Web sessions you will encounter at least some sites for which access is either impossible or unacceptably slow. This does *not* necessarily indicate that there is anything wrong with your computer, or your connection to the Internet - it is just currently a fact of digital life. Once you understand and allow for this, it need not detract too severely from your use and enjoyment of the Web.

The other bad news about the Web runs a little deeper, and may take rather longer to improve. I have already referred to it in passing: it is the problem of low quality content.

Remember first of all that most of the information resources currently offered on the World Wide Web are free of any special access charge. This is, once you have paid your ISP, and your phone bill, there is no further charge for accessing particular resources.

Now the publishers of information on the Web do not receive any payment from either the ISPs or the phone companies. So there is very limited immediate incentive and ability for publishers to invest in the production of high quality materials. This is very different from more traditional publishing media, such as books, newspapers, TV etc., where the (successful) publisher receives a direct payment from each consumer.

Perversely, this situation is made worse by the fact that the "production" cost of electronic publication (as opposed to authoring or development cost) is very small. As noted in the previous chapter, most ISPs actually offer a facility to host, or publish, a certain amount of information as part of their standard account. To put it crudely, cranks and crackpots can - for very moderate cost - use the Web as a medium to make their craziest ideas available to a global audience. Mind you, this is still subject to all normal publication laws in any particular jurisdiction, such as laws regulating publication of obscene or defamatory information, and laws relating to republication of copyrighted materials etc. Nonetheless, that still leaves a lot of space for crackpottery. Furthermore, legal systems vary greatly between different countries. Because of the global nature of the Internet there will be some materials which, though legal and even commonplace in their countries of publication, may be illegal, or at least seriously offensive, in various other countries where they can be accessed.

The nett result of all these factors is that the quality of Web information resources varies very widely indeed.

You should certainly *not* assume that, just because information is being relayed to you via this high-tech computerised system, it must therefore be true, or well-founded, or even grammatically expressed! Be prepared to come across an awful lot of chaff mixed in with a relatively modest amount of wheat. Perhaps even more than any previous publication medium, the Web requires the information users or consumers to exercise their own independent critical judgment. This means you!

Having said that, the situation is by no means completely bleak. There are many situations where high quality information is available on the Web, despite the fact that there is no direct recompense for the publisher.

The most obvious incentive for providing high quality information is where this can be associated with promotion or advertising. Many companies are taking to making useful information resources or services freely available on the Web so as to entice you to visit their sites, and thus be also exposed to some advertising message. There are also independent content sites, funded by advertising, in the manner of online newspapers or magazines - an excellent Irish example is the *IOL Leisure* site, which can be accessed via the IOL portal at:*:

```
http://www.iol.ie/
```

Then there are the many public service organisations which have a specific mission (or even obligation) to disseminate useful information to the widest possible audience. In this category we have organisations such as state departments and agencies, museums, universities and research institutions, charities, political parties,

Welcome Aboard

What Is This Internet Thing Anyway

Your Net Computer

Getting On-line

The Web

E-mail

Other Internet Services

Welcome Aboard

What Is This Internet Thing Anyway

Your Net Computer

Getting On-line

The Web

E-mail

Other Internet Services

and so on. These organisations are increasingly seeing the Web as a powerful new way of extending the reach of their publications, at very little additional cost.

Finally, there are many, many groups and individuals who publish high quality, useful, information resources simply because they are interested in it, enjoy doing it, appreciate the global contacts it introduces them to - and not at all for any monetary reward to themselves. In this category we have clubs, societies, charities, hobby groups and a wealth of others.

It also cannot be emphasised too much that the Web is expanding and developing at an extraordinary rate. The generalisations made here about the quality of the information available on the Web will be at least somewhat out of date before this book is even printed. We'll return to look at some of the newest developments in Internet technology (as well as some of the oldest!) in chapter 6 - especially that most talked about buzzword of *e-commerce*. But first, it's time to step back to something simpler and more mundane. That is the modern rebirth of the old fashioned letter, in the new guise of electronic mail or *e-mail*.

5. E-Mail: Letters Make a Comeback

E lectronic mail - e-mail - was one of the first applications of the Internet. It simply means the ability to send letters "electronically", down the phone line, rather than the old fashioned way with pen, ink and pony express.

E-mail does not receive nearly as much media hype as the Web. It generally does not involve fancy graphics, video, or animations. Nor has it accumulated so much mystifying jargon. E-mail is also relatively cheap in that it typically requires much less time online, accumulating call charges, compared to Web browsing.

And yet, e-mail is probably still the single most useful facility the Internet has to offer. Even if you never bother with browsing the Web, e-mail on its own may well justify all the effort and cost of connecting to the Internet.

The Pros ...

How is e-mail such an improvement over the good old paper-based postal system?

Firstly, e-mail is *fast*. Even if you already use a computer to write letters, this involves printing them out on paper, printing labels for the envelopes, sealing and stamping, and finally delivery to a postbox or post office. With e-mail, once you have composed the text of a letter, it can be sent at the click of a button. There is no printing, no envelope, no stamp, no stroll to the post office - just click the button and everything else is automatic.

Even more impressively, actual delivery of e-mail is usually almost instantaneous. The transfer of an e-mail on the Internet normally requires no more than a few seconds, regardless of where on the planet it is coming from or going to. In exceptional circumstances it might take a few hours - still much less than any paper-based delivery system can aspire to. The main delay between sending an e-mail and its being read at the other end is nothing to do with the Internet: it is the time that elapses until the person at the receiving end checks their electronic "mailbox" for new e-mail.

Now you can see why afficionados of e-mail have invented the term *snail-mail* for conventional paper-based post!

If speed were the only consideration, one might think that the telephone would score every time over e-mail, but think again. Speed is *not* the only consideration. For

Welcome Aboard

What Is This Internet Thing Anyway

Your Net Computer

Getting On-line

The Web

E-mail

Other Internet Services

Welcome Aboard

What Is This Internet Thing Anyway

Your Net Computer

Getting On-line

The Web

E-mail

Other Internet Services

anything other than local calls, e-mail is much cheaper than telephoning. It also has all the traditional advantages of *writing* over speech. E-mail is durable, it provides a semi-permanent record of a discussion. E-mail does not require both people to participate simultaneously. And e-mail gives you the time to compose your communication carefully, and so communicate your message more effectively.

The second great advantage of e-mail is that it is as easy to send a message to ten people, or one hundred people, as to just one. E-mail is an electronic format, and so the computer can easily duplicate it, as many times as you want. You can copy that same party invitation to all your friends; or circulate the agenda for the AGM to all the members of your parents' association, or bridge club. Of course, this relies on all the people you want to communicate with having access to e-mail, but I will return to that question a little later.

Finally, because e-mail is already electronic, it is extremely easy to keep organised records of all your correspondence, both incoming and outgoing, actually on your computer. This quickly becomes a lot more compact than using a tower of shoeboxes or investing in a filing cabinet. More importantly, your computer can easily and quickly search through the text of *every* e-mail message you have on file, to find a particular subject or person. So even if you don't sort your correspondence carefully, or even if you accidentally misfile an important message, you still have an excellent chance of finding it.

... And The Cons!

Of course, e-mail has a few *disadvantages* also.

First, as I noted, e-mail is only useful for communicating with other people who use e-mail. Although interest in the Internet has exploded in the past number of years, the fact remains that many, many people do not have access. This particularly limits applications such as circulating information for a local club or association: e-mail should be extremely handy for this, but if even two or three of the people involved do not have e-mail, it becomes much less useful.

On the other hand, we can reasonably expect that this is only a temporary limitation. E-mail is now reaching the same sort of "take-off" point that fax communication reached some years ago. But whereas the fax revolution was largely limited to business communication, it looks like e-mail will penetrate quickly and deeply into personal correspondence. For example, many students in third level educational institutions automatically have access to e-mail. This is a strong incentive for parents and friends to also acquire e-mail access. Further, as these students graduate, they are likely to continue their use of e-mail.

Note also that 100% e-mail access does not necessarily mean that every household must have an Internet computer and connection of its own. Those who don't need or want this full service could still avail of a personal e-mail service, via access in a local library, cybercafé, or even post office - in fact any location where public access Internet terminals or kiosks may be made available. A number of organisations, such as *IOL*, offer *free* Internet mailboxes, which can be accessed from any Internet terminal via a Web browser. This is a sort of modern day reincarnation of the traditional PO Box and *poste restante* services, whereby people without a fixed physical postal address can still receive their mail.

OK, so let us suppose that, even if not quite everyone you want to write to already has e-mail, they soon will. Despite this, there are still some other significant problems with the use of e-mail.

I have already explained that e-mail makes it very easy (and cheap) to send copies of a single message to many, many recipients and that there are situations in which this is very useful - but this is also, unfortunately, a strong temptation for the purveyors of "junk" e-mail. So alongside the general growth of the Internet in the past few years, there has been a matching, or even faster, growth in the transmission of *unsolicited* e-mail (also known as "spam" e-mail). Perhaps not quite all of this qualifies as "junk", but, in my experience, the vast majority does. It is a genuine and growing problem. But, unlike with the conventional postal system, there may be technological means to curtail this anti-social phenomenon. "E-mail filtering" technology allows your computer to reject, or silently delete, e-mail from specified or unrecognised sources, or based on various other criteria. There are also moves by the ISPs to control the use of their facilities for junk e-mail. From their point of view, this is a parasitic activity that uses their service - they are *not* receiving any special payment from the originators of this junk e-mail. There may also be some attempt at legal control of junk e-mail, though the prospects for success there are limited because of the international nature of the Internet.

In any case, I will take the opportunity to caution you here against the many "get-rich quick" schemes that you will inevitably receive e-mail about. In general these are nothing more than electronic versions of old-fashioned pyramid scams. They will certainly not make you rich. Even to participate in them is probably illegal.

The final problem which I will mention regarding e-mail is that of *privacy*. Internet e-mail, in its current form, is fundamentally insecure. It is relatively easy for your e-mail to be intercepted, tapped, diverted, modified, or even for e-mail to be originated in your name without your permission or knowledge. The equipment and technical knowledge required is relatively modest. Unauthorised access to your e-mail correspondence is probably a lot easier than to your conventional paper post or to yout telephone conversations. This applies to potential access by "legitimate" law

Welcome Aboard

What Is This Internet Thing Anyway

Your Net Computer

Getting On-line

The Web

E-mail

Other Internet Services

Welcome Aboard

What Is This Internet Thing Anyway

Your Net Computer

Getting On-line

The Web

E-mail

Other Internet Services

enforcement agencies, by the media, by nosey or intrusive individuals, and by malicious or criminal individuals or organisations, in Ireland or abroad. It is widely believed that certain "intelligence" agencies in countries around the world *routinely* scan all internationally routed e-mail for key words and phrases. This is difficult to corroborate - by definition - but it is certainly *technically* feasible.

Again, the situation is not completely bleak. There are already technological solutions to these problems, methods for "encoding" or "encrypting" your communications so that only the intended recipient can read them; and of electronically signing messages so that the recipient can be sure that the communication came from you and nobody else. Unfortunately, there are still many competing technological solutions, at least some of which are not *really* secure. This is a technically difficult area, and it is not reasonable to expect individual Internet users to be able to assess the merits of the different schemes. In any case, the lack of standardisation is a big barrier: even if you have identified a good encryption system, this will not be effective in protecting your e-mail communication unless all the people you want to communicate with have access to a compatible system.

An additional complication is that the legality of the use of various kinds of encryption is not completely clear. For many years, the US has regarded encryption software as a form of "munition" (!) and subject to export controls. Various other countries (including some "democracies") actually outlaw the use of encryption within their jurisdictions. In complete contrast, there are also countries which have enshrined a constitutionally guaranteed right to the privacy of their citizens' communications (electronic or otherwise). So the regulatory and standardisation situation with regard to Internet security is currently quite unsatisfactory.

While various efforts are underway to address these issues, I recommend that you should *not* use unencrypted Internet e-mail for any communication which you consider private or confidential. Conversely, if you do wish to use encrypted e-mail, you should seek *independent* professional advice as to the adequacy of any particular product for your purposes. The following Web site provides much more detailed information on these and related issues:

```
http://www.interhack.net/people/cmcurtin/snake-oil-faq.html
```

The following Google directory provides references for various encryption related products and services:

```
http://directory.google.com/Top/Computers/Security/
        Products_and_Tools/Cryptography/
```

The Online/Offline Issue

When your computer is actually on the phone, connected to your ISP, you are said to be *online*. Conversely, when your computer is not on the phone you are *offline*.

Clearly, while you are offline your access to the Internet is pretty restricted! On the other hand, online time generally costs money, in the form of call charges. Perhaps more importantly, being online means that you cannot receive incoming phone calls - unless you have more than one phone line, or perhaps have a mobile as well as a fixed phone connection. I can vouch for the latter problem being the biggest single complaint against Internet usage in my own household! So it would be very convenient if at least some Internet activities could be carried out while you are offline. And as it turns out this is indeed possible, at least up to a point. I have already briefly referred to this in discussing Web browsing. There I noted that once you were viewing a Web page in your browser, you could hang up the phone connection while you settled back to read it. You could even save the page in a file stored on your hard disk, so that you could come back and view it at any later time without going online.

This is useful so far as it goes, but it is pretty limited. In particular, while you are offline embedded images in a page may not display correctly. More importantly, you will not generally be able to follow links from a page to other pages. There is technology on the horizon which attempts to improve this situation. In effect this tries to anticipate what Web pages you are "likely" to want to view, and spontaneously downloads them whenever you happen to be online. This can be made to happen automatically regardless of whether you explicitly request these pages *while* online. Subsequently, when you are offline, you may still be able to do some worthwhile browsing, because these materials have already been downloaded to your machine in advance. This sounds useful, but it also has significant limitations. It cannot apply, for example, to streaming media (live audio or video broadcasts), or to other interactive activities (submitting a query to a search engine etc.). And the "anticipations" of what you will want to browse may well be mistaken. This can mean both that materials you want are not available when you are offline, and also that extra, wasteful, Internet traffic is generated while you are online, downloading materials that you never subsequently refer to. This causes extra undesirable costs and delays both for yourself and for other Internet users. So while we can expect some continuing incremental improvements in this technology, it seems that effective Web access will continue to rely in large measure on actually being online.

The long-term technological solution to this will probably be to go in a completely different direction. There are at least two possibilities. First is a new kind of phone connection that can effectively carry data at any time, on demand, without having to make a conventional "telephone" call, and without interfering in any way with conventional phone calls (incoming or outgoing). As usual, there is a new acronym

Welcome Aboard

What Is This Internet Thing Anyway

Your Net Computer

Getting On-line

The Web

E-mail

Other Internet Services

Welcome Aboard

What Is This Internet Thing Anyway

Your Net Computer

Getting On-line

The Web

E-mail

Other Internet Services

to describe this: ADSL or *Asynchronous Digital Subscriber Loop*. ADSL would mean that your computer and your phone would share the same wires to your local telephone exchange, without interfering with each other. Your computer would be permanently connected to the Internet, but your phone would still be simultaneously usable for "normal" telephone calls. The second possibility would be to use cable TV networks, or perhaps even electricity networks, to carry Internet data. Either of these kinds of Internet service would likely be charged on a *flat rate* basis (i.e., subscription fee only, with no "call" charges). For good measure, they would both allow data to be transferred between you and your ISP at much faster rates than is possible on standard phone lines. However, all of these systems would require very substantial new investment before they could become widely available.

So, for the immediate future at least, you will still want to control your online time. I have explained that, in the case of Web browsing, there are definite limits to doing that. The situation with e-mail is - potentially at least - quite different. The way it works is this. You have two main activities in dealing with e-mail: you compose new messages to send out, and you review (read, reply to, file etc.) messages you receive. An e-mail client (a special program which you use on your local computer to access e-mail) can allow you to do almost all of this while you are offline. That is, you can compose new outgoing messages, read through messages you have previously received, rearrange them, and compose new replies. Of course, your outgoing messages cannot really be sent since you are offline. Instead, they will be stored in a queue, on your computer, waiting until you are online. Similarly, new messages arriving for you will not really be able to get to you while you are offline. Instead, they will just get as far as your ISP's e-mail server, where they will again be entered in a queue, waiting to be finally delivered to you. This incoming queue, held on the ISP's e-mail server, is often also called your incoming *mailbox*. Now, when you choose, you go online. Your e-mail client then relays all the messages in the outgoing queue to the e-mail server, and collects all new incoming messages from the e-mail server, thus emptying both queues. As soon as that is completed, you can go offline again. If you do this reasonably regularly, say once a day, or every couple of days, neither queue will be very big, so your actual online time on each occasion need typically be no more than a few minutes. Furthermore, you can choose to do it at whatever times of the day call charges are at a minimum. In this way, the vast majority of the time you spend using or dealing with e-mail can be offline time.

The detailed discussion below will generally assume that you are using e-mail in this mainly offline mode. However, I should note that there is an alternative to this. This is to not store or process e-mail on your local computer at all, but, instead, to use a Web-based e-mail service, accessed through your normal Web browser rather than via a special e-mail client program. By definition, you must be online for much longer periods to use this kind of service - but it can have other distinct advantages of its own. I will discuss this approach a little further at the end of the chapter.

E-mail Addresses

E-mail addresses - like Web URLs - have a fairly standardised format. Here's an example:

```
BarryMcMullin@iolfree.ie
```

This consists of two parts, separated by the @ (pronounced "at") character. The part on the right is called the *domain*. It is similar to the host or server name in a URL. It identifies the permanently connected server computer that accepts e-mail for this person - i.e., where his or her electronic "mailbox" is located.

Since any given e-mail server computer will normally accept e-mail for many different people, the part of the e-mail address to the left of the @ symbol identifies one particular user. It is technically called the *username* part. Usually this is some kind of shortened version of the person's full name, or perhaps a generic code for a department. Here are a few more examples:

```
AskBill@microsoft.com
Editor@irish-times.com
Marian@rte.ie
President@whitehouse.gov
Help@esatfusion.ie
```

E-mail addresses must always contain exactly one @ symbol. In general, it does not matter whether characters in e-mail addresses are typed in capital or small letters (for example, President@WhiteHouse.gov and preSiDenT@whitehouse.GOV will both be delivered to the same place). E-mail addresses are also often encountered in a slightly more longwinded form, like this:

```
Marian Finucane <Marian@rte.ie>
```

In this case the e-mail address consists of the person's full name together with the address "proper", as I have already discussed, set off by angle brackets "<" and ">". You will often see this form of address in e-mail you receive. It is useful because the shorthand name (username) part of the address proper may be a bit cryptic.

Your own e-mail address(es) will be arranged in consultation with your ISP. Depending on the ISP, and the particular service you have selected from them, you will be eligible for at least one e-mail address, but may well want more. The advantage of getting several separate e-mail addresses is that the different members of your household can each independently manage their own e-mail. *IOL* offers an unlimited number of free e-mail addresses to all its users.

Welcome Aboard

What Is This Internet Thing Anyway

Your Net Computer

Getting On-line

The Web

E-mail

Other Internet Services

Welcome
Aboard

What Is This Internet
Thing Anyway

Your Net
Computer

Getting On-line

The Web

E-mail

Other Internet
Services

For personal Internet accounts, the domain in your e-mail address will normally be a standard domain associated with the ISP, such as `iolfree.ie` for the ***IOL Free*** service. You will usually have some degree of choice in the username part of an e-mail address. Associated with each e-mail address there will also be a *password*, to control access to incoming e-mail for that address. If you are getting just a single e-mail address, the username and password may be the same as those controlling overall connection to the ISP, though that need not necessarily be the case.

Of course, to start using e-mail in earnest, you will need e-mail addresses for people you want to contact. It would be very convenient if there were the e-mail equivalent of the telephone directory where you could look this up. There *are* a number of e-mail directory services, available via the Web, but their coverage is patchy. As a beginner you should probably rely on directly asking people you know for their own e-mail addresses, through meeting them, calling them on the phone, or even via snail mail. For contacting businesses by e-mail it's usually best to try and find a web site for the business first. If they accept correspondence by e-mail, they will surely *have* a web site, and will give the relevant addresses there. Over time you will easily build up your own personal e-mail "address book". Better yet, as we shall see, your personal e-mail address book can be stored in electronic form on your computer, which makes it very easy to use and maintain.

Your E-mail Client Program

Just as with Web browsing, you will need a suitable software package or program to support your access to e-mail (unless, as mentioned, you opt for a Web based e-mail service, in which case you will simply use your Web browser for e-mail also). This is called your e-mail *client* program. Again, there are a number of different packages available, with various prices and facilities. The software suite provided by ***IOL*** on the accompanying CD-ROM includes *Microsoft Outlook Express*, or MS–OE for short, and I will use it here for illustration. I will also again assume that the client is installed under the Microsoft Windows Operating System. The general capabilities and operation of other e-mail clients, such as *Netscape Messenger* (included in the *Communicator* suite), or clients running under other operating systems, will be very similar.

Client Configuration

Your e-mail client program must be configured with certain personalized information about you and your ISP. It is useful to have some understanding of what kind of information is required, and the related jargon. This will be handy when first setting up the client, and also if you want to change the configuration, or even change to a different e-mail client, at a later date.

When you first start up MS–OE, a configuration "wizard" will automatically appear to prompt you for the required information. Some of this information may already be

Welcome Aboard

What Is This Internet Thing Anyway

Your Net Computer

Getting On-line

The Web

E-mail

Other Internet Services

correctly pre-configured, but you should nonetheless check it carefully. If several people share the computer, but with their own individual e-mail addresses, they will each have to separately configure their own information with MS-OE. You can arrange this by configuring separate user "accounts" within MS-OE, and/or by configuring completely separate users for Windows. If you ever need to check or modify the MS-OE configuration information, you can do so by clicking on the Tools menu, and then clicking on Accounts. Consult the MS-OE electronic help for more detailed information.

The key e-mail configuration information for a single user's e-mail account is as follows:

Full name. This will be shown, along with your e-mail address proper, on any messages you send. Your full name will make it easier for the people who receive your e-mail to identify the sender, because your e-mail address proper may be somewhat cryptic.

Your e-mail address. You must enter this *exactly* as arranged with your ISP. Any mistake may not be apparent to you, but it will mean that when people attempt to reply to e-mail they receive from you the reply will not be routed correctly and you will never receive it.

Your e-mail servers. These are the Internet names for the server computers that handle your e-mail. The names will be specified by your ISP, and will normally be recognisable as belonging to the ISP. Most e-mail clients require you to configure servers for outgoing and incoming e-mail separately, though these may both be handled by the same machine. In the case of *IOL Free*, for example, the incoming mail server is pop.iolfree.ie, and mail.iolfree.ie handles outgoing mail. The outgoing server may also be referred to as the *SMTP* server. SMTP

Welcome Aboard

What Is This Internet Thing Anyway

Your Net Computer

Getting On-line

The Web

E-mail

Other Internet Services

stands for "Simple Mail Transfer Protocol". For historical and technical reasons, most Internet e-mail clients used with temporary (dial-up) Internet access, use SMTP only for outgoing e-mail. Incoming e-mail is most commonly handled by a different protocol, called POP3 ("Post Office Protocol Version 3") or, possibly, IMAP ("Internet Message Access Protocol"). If this is not already pre-configured, your ISP will advise you which is supported or recommended.

Your e-mail "username" and "password". These are used to control fetching of your incoming e-mail from its temporary mailbox on the ISP's incoming e-mail server. Note that this password controls only the *downloading* of incoming e-mail: once the e-mail is located on your computer it is *not* protected by this password. The MS–OE configuration wizard does request this password, but it may be left blank, in which case MS–OE will request the password only as and when it is needed, rather than recording it permanently.

The configuration wizard will run automatically only the first time you start up MS–OE, but you can run it again at any time via the **Add** button on the **Accounts** dialog box (accessed through the **Tools** menu).

MS–OE also has a large range of additional options which allow you to tailor its behaviour to suit your own preferences. These can be accessed via the **Options** item on the **Tools** menu, You should explore their effects when you feel more comfortable with the general behaviour of the package.

Anatomy Of An E-mail Client

Each time you start MS–OE afresh it may query you on whether to immediately go online; however, for the moment I will assume that you cancel this and remain offline for at least the initial part of your MS–OE session. As with your first look at the Microsoft Internet Explorer browser window, your first experience of the main MS–OE window may be a little intimidating. But once you pick out the key elements it will seem much more understandable.

Your e-mail messages will be stored in e-mail *folders*. You can have as many folders as you like. You can even nest folders within folders. You can move messages around between folders, or copy them so that you can have copies of the same message in multiple folders (no more agonising over which is the more appropriate place to file a particular letter: you can put copies in both places!).

A number of folders are automatically created when MS–OE is installed. Inbox is where all newly arrived messages, i.e., newly downloaded from your ISP, will arrive. Outbox queues up messages you have composed, ready for transmission via your ISP.

`Sent Items` is used to hold copies of messages you have sent, for your own reference. `Drafts` holds any partial messages you have started to compose, but have not committed for sending yet. Finally, `Deleted Items` is a little like the main Windows *Recycle Bin* and serves to hold messages which you have indicated should be deleted; messages can still be retrieved ("undeleted") while they are in `Deleted Items` - but once this is emptied any messages here are *permanently* deleted (and their disk space freed up again).

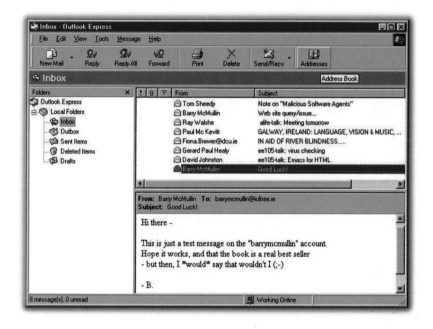

Now let's examine the main `MS-OE` window systematically from top to bottom. You will notice some similarities with the Microsoft Internet Explorer window - indeed, similarities with many applications designed for the Microsoft Windows environment.

At the top is the window *Title Bar*, with the usual buttons for resizing or closing, and the application name (*Outlook Express*). Below the title bar is the *Menu Bar*. As usual, if you click on any of the words here, a menu of possible further actions will drop down.

Next comes the *Tool Bar*. As with the `MS-IE` Browser Tool Bar, this is a collection of buttons that give quick access to certain operations that are used frequently. Precisely what buttons are displayed here may change dynamically according to the context of what you are doing (e.g., additional buttons become available when you are viewing a specific message). Again, there is a special *Activity* icon at the extreme right

Welcome Aboard

What Is This Internet Thing Anyway

Your Net Computer

Getting On-line

The Web

E-mail

Other Internet Services

Welcome
Aboard

What Is This Internet
Thing Anyway

Your Net
Computer

Getting On-line

The Web

E-mail

Other Internet
Services

of the Tool Bar which will become animated to indicate Internet communication. Below this, the window is divided into a number of separate panes. On the left is the *Folder List*. Clicking on a particular folder will select it for display, causing the *Message List* and *Preview Pane* for that folder to appear to the right. The Message List shows a summary of all the messages in the currently selected folder (i.e., the folder selected in the Folder List). The list is organised in a number of columns, showing the message originator, the subject heading and date and time received. Depending on the MS-OE configuration there may be additional columns such as the size of each message, whom it was addressed to, and the date and time sent.

When you first start up MS-OE there may be one or more "dummy" messages already in your Inbox. These will be promotional messages from Microsoft, pointing out some of the features of MS-OE. Unless there is some information here that you particularly want to retain you can probably safely delete them.

Once you start sending and receiving your own e-mail messages, the message lists for your various folders will become longer and it may not be possible to show all the messages within the available space. Whenever that happens a scroll bar will appear on the right-hand side of the Message List pane, allowing you to scroll up or down through a long message list.

The Preview Pane shows the content of whichever message (if any) is currently selected in the Message List. Again, a scroll bar will appear on the right-hand side, if necessary, to allow scrolling through the message.

Finally, at the bottom of the window is a *Status Bar*. This is used to display summary status information about the folder (such as how many messages it contains, and how many have not yet been read), and progress of operations such as sending or receiving new e-mail.

Sending Your First E-mail Message

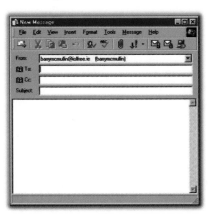

Now it's time to send your first outgoing e-mail message. Click on the **New Mail** button in the Tool Bar. This will bring up a separate window for message composition. This has its own Menu Bar and Tool Bar tailored for the composition job. It also has two other panes, the upper one for header or cover information relating to your message, and the lower one for the message itself.

The header pane has spaces or "fields" for four separate pieces of information: who to send the message `To:`, who to send extra copies to, under two separate headings `Cc:` and `Bcc:`, and finally, the message `Subject:`. In general you should click on each of these in turn and enter the required information (if any). The `To:` field should contain the e-mail address of the "primary" recipient of the message. If you wish, you can enter multiple e-mail addresses, separated by comma `","` characters. `Cc:` stands for "carbon copy" - which is a marvelously obscure throwback to a much older messaging technology! The idea is that if there are people to whom the message is not directly addressed, but who would benefit from having a copy, their addresses can be listed in the `Cc:` field. The `Bcc:` field stands for "blind carbon copy". It is similar to the `Cc:` field except that the recipients will not be able to see who else was listed under `Bcc:`. Again, multiple addresses can be entered in each of the `Cc:` and `Bcc:` fields, separated by comma characters.

For your first experiment in e-mail, click on the `To:` field and fill in your *own* e-mail address.

Why send e-mail to yourself? Well, this is the one e-mail address that you should definitely know. By sending e-mail to this address, and checking that it does indeed get delivered to your `Inbox,` you will be able to verify all aspects of your e-mail configuration. You will also ensure that you have *got* the correct e-mail address for yourself. It is best to check that this is so before you send e-mail to anyone else, because otherwise they may not be able to reply to you (and you will not have any indication of this).

Next click on the `Subject:` field. This should contain a short title or reference for your message, indicating what it is about. This is common in conventional business correspondence, but not so common in personal letters. Nonetheless, you should get into the habit of filling this in, even on personal messages. As we have already seen, subject headings will be displayed in the message list when you are viewing the main `MS-OE` window. Similar summary views of folders will be available with all e-mail clients. Good, appropriate, subject lines, make it much easier to sort and organise incoming e-mail - so using the subject line sensibly is really a matter of courtesy to the person who will receive the e-mail.

For your first message, a sensible `Subject:` field might be something like:

```
My first e-mail message!
```

Now you can click on the bottom pane where you can enter the text of your message. This is really just like a small, simple, word processor.

By default `MS-OE` normally allows messages to be formatted in HTML - like a web page. This allows a variety of formatting effects such as different character sizes or

Welcome Aboard

What Is This Internet Thing Anyway

Your Net Computer

Getting On-line

The Web

E-mail

Other Internet Services

Welcome Aboard

What Is This Internet Thing Anyway

Your Net Computer

Getting On-line

The Web

E-mail

Other Internet Services

styles (italic, boldface, etc.), as well as embedded hyperlinks etc. You may already have seen an example of this in the dummy message from Microsoft loaded in the Inbox folder. However, this facility will only work properly if the person who receives the message *also* has an e-mail client that can handle HTML messages. This will be true of MS-OE and of Netscape Messenger - but is not true of many other e-mail clients in widespread use on the Internet. Furthermore, it is my experience that, if formatting facilities are available, many people become almost addicted to them, investing quite inordinate amounts of time in playing with the *appearance* of a message rather than concentrating on its *content*. So I recommend that you compose e-mail messages in HTML *only* if you have some very definite requirement for its more advanced formatting capability, *and* you are sure that all recipients of the message will be able to display HTML. In all other cases you should compose messages in so-called *plain text*.

"Plain text" is also often referred to as *ASCII* text, which stands for "American Standard Code for Information Interchange". ASCII is quite a mouthful but it is one buzzword worth remembering, because it a sort of lowest common denominator of the computer world: practically every computer in the world is capable of correctly handling information in this format. So if you compose your e-mail message in ASCII you are pretty well guaranteed that the recipients will be able to read it, no matter what type of computer they use, and no matter what program they use for accessing e-mail. You can select the ASCII format for any single message in MS-OE by clicking on Plain Text in the Format menu. Better still, you can make this your default for all new messages via the Options dialog box (click Options on the Tools menu of the main MS-OE window).

Now type in a few lines of text - anything at all will do, just for test purposes. When the message is ready, send it by clicking on the **Send** button in the Tool Bar of the composition window.

If you happen to be already online, the message will be transferred to your ISP's mail server and then delivered onward (in this case just to your own mailbox on the ISP's server). If you are not already online MS-OE will either cause your computer to go online so that it can transfer the message *immediately*, or it will queue the message up in the Outbox folder for the time being. As already discussed, the latter behaviour is generally preferable because it means you can accumulate all the messages which you want to send so that they can be transferred together in one efficient online session. If this is not the default behaviour (i.e., if MS-OE goes online immediately) you can again change this via the main MS-OE Options dialog box.

In any case, the e-mail composition window now disappears, and you will be left with the MS-OE main window again. If the message has just been queued, you might take a moment to switch to the Outbox folder in the Folder List. You should be able

Welcome Aboard

What Is This Internet Thing Anyway

Your Net Computer

Getting On-line

The Web

E-mail

Other Internet Services

to see your message, queued and waiting to be sent. You do not *have* to check the Outbox at this stage: but it is generally a good idea to briefly review your outgoing e-mail before it is finally sent. This is a further advantage of queueing up outgoing messages - even at this stage, you can change your mind about the content of a message, or whether to send it at all. To re-edit a queued message, double click on it in the Outbox message list, and it will reappear in a message composition window. When you have finished making changes, click on the send button and the revised message will be put back into the Outbox folder. (Alternatively, if you decide you would prefer not to send a message after all, just click once on it in the Message List, to select or highlight it, and then click on the **Delete** button ✖ in the Tool Bar.)

Well, now we are ready to commit ourselves. Click on the **Send/Recv** button 📧 on the Tool Bar. This will cause your computer to go online, and establish the telephone connection to your ISP in just the same way as when you start up MS-IE. If necessary, provide any required information (such as your connection password) and click on OK in the dialup connection dialog box. The connection will be established as normal.

You may or may not be prompted to enter your e-mail account password: this depends on whether you entered the password when you configured this account into MS-OE. If you are prompted, enter the password now. Note again that the information required is your *e-mail* username and password - which is not necessarily the same as your connection username and password. If you *are* prompted for this information, it means that MS-OE is not configured to permanently record it. Nonetheless, MS-OE will only request the information once each session. Now a window will appear reporting the progress of emptying the outgoing and incoming e-mail queues (this will also be reflected in the status bar at the bottom of the main MS-OE window). First, any queued outgoing messages are sent, then any incoming messages waiting at your ISP are downloaded to your Inbox folder. In our particular case, there is just one ongoing message. Typically, the processing of this will be fast enough so that by the time MS-OE switches to check for incoming messages, your own message will already be waiting and will be downloaded. Change to viewing the Inbox to check this. If it has not arrived, wait a few seconds and then click on Send and Receive again. Your first message should then arrive.

You should find that, by default, MS-OE does *not* automatically hang up the telephone connection to your ISP immediately after it has completed sending and receiving. This is because, if you immediately review your incoming e-mail, you may decide that there are one or two messages that you should quickly and briefly reply to. These replies can then be dispatched using the same connection, which is to say the same phone call. This also allows you to combine dealing with e-mail and doing some Web browsing within one telephone call. On the other hand, it will more usually be the case that you want to take your time reading and thinking about the messages you have received, and composing replies. In this case, you can shut down the connection as soon as MS-OE is finished emptying the current queues. If you exit the MS-OE program you will normally be prompted to do this anyway. If you want to terminate the connection without exiting from MS-OE, double click on the connection icon in your Windows Task Bar, usually at the bottom right hand corner of your screen. You will then get a dialog box where you can cause a disconnection.

Once you have managed to send a message to yourself, and have successfully received it, you will have mastered the essential elements of using e-mail. You are ready and able to start exchanging e-mail with anybody whose e-mail address you know or can find out. Indeed, I recommend that you go ahead and do precisely this. Build up your familiarity with using this exciting new variation on a very old communications medium, without worrying *too* much about the many other bells and whistles which e-mail clients may have to offer. However, when you *are* ready for them, the bells and whistles can be pretty useful. In the remaining sections of this chapter I will briefly review some of the other facilities available with MS-OE.

Replying And Forwarding

As you establish contacts by e-mail, you will find that much of the e-mail you compose will be in the form of responses to e-mails you have received. MS-OE offers three buttons on the Tool Bar to help with this. In each case I assume that you have selected or highlighted some particular message before clicking on one of these buttons.

 Reply: This creates a new message composition window. The new message is automatically addressed to the person who originated the message to you in the first place. You can add more recipients, in the To:, Cc:, or Bcc: fields, if you wish. Note carefully that the address automatically used in replying *may* be different from the address of the actual originator - and thus may not be the address you intended. There are few e-mail experiences more embarrassing than sending a caustic message to the wrong address. Therefore, when using the Reply button you should *always* explicitly check the To: field to be sure it is as you expected. If not, manually re-edit it. The Subject: field will be automatically filled in with the same subject as the original message, prefixed with Re:, indicating to the recipient that this message *is* a reply or continuation of a previous correspondence.

The new window will also contain a copy of the text of the original message, indented slightly and with a special character (usually ">") at the start of each line. In e-mail jargon, this is said to be a "quoted" version of the original message. The idea here is that, in composing a reply, you will typically want to refer to the text of the original message you received. You could simply retype, and/or rephrase the relevant part of the original. Indeed, that is how traditional paper-based letters were written. But with e-mail it is trivially easy to electronically copy the original text, and that is

Welcome Aboard

What Is This Internet Thing Anyway

Your Net Computer

Getting On-line

The Web

E-mail

Other Internet Services

Welcome Aboard

What Is This Internet Thing Anyway

Your Net Computer

Getting On-line

The Web

E-mail

Other Internet Services

what has been done here. The normal way of using this quoted text is to intersperse your responses within it. Since the lines of your own reply text will not be "quoted" (not indented with a ">" character), it will be easy for the recipient of the reply to distinguish between quotation and your new comments. This is actually a very neat and handy way of working, once you get used to it - and, of course, it need not stop at one level of replying. The person you reply to may reply to that in turn. In that case, the original text will become doubly quoted (doubly indented, with double ">" characters on each line), your reply text would be singly indented, and the second level reply would be unquoted. If the correspondence continues further, even further levels of quoting can arise.

However, there is an obvious problem here. Suppose you simply leave in all the original text, as well as your new comments, whenever you write a reply. If the correspondence goes back and forth several times it will accumulate *all* the text of all the messages, in a very convoluted, multiply quoted format. This quickly becomes virtually impossible to make sense of any more.

The solution is to use the quoting mechanism *sparingly*. Just because all the text of the original message has been automatically placed in quoted form into your reply composition window, does *not* mean that you have to leave it there. Instead, delete any of it that does not directly relate to, or clarify, your reply. Delete *all* of it if you like. As a rule of thumb, in any reply, there should be at least as much new text as there is quoted text from the original message - and preferably a good deal more. As you will quickly find out for yourself, the presence of an excess of quoted text in messages makes them extremely hard to read. This is considered to be positively *rude*. If you want to use e-mail effectively it is best to develop an early habit of ruthlessly pruning quoted text.

 Reply All: This is identical to **Reply** except that *all* of the original recipients will be automatically addressed in the new message composition window, not just the originator. This makes it easier to ensure that, if a number of people receive copies of an e-mail, they will also all receive copies of a reply. However, as with the **Reply** button, you should not *trust* that the correct addresses have been automatically entered. Rather, you should check that the addressees are as you expect, and re-edit them if necessary.

Forward: The effect of this button is again to create a new message composition window, with the original message quoted within it. However, *no* addressees are automatically entered, and the prefix Fw: is added to the Subject: field instead of Re:. The idea, of course, is that this allows you to conveniently forward a message to another person, not among the original recipients. In this case, although MS-OE does quote the original message, it will still all be "new" text to the recipient, so that the earlier cautions about removing excess quoted text do not apply. (Indeed, many other mail clients would not quote the text of a forwarded message at all, which arguably makes more sense!)

It is a good idea, early on in your experiments with e-mail, to address a dummy e-mail to yourself as already described, and then, when it arrives, use the **Reply** button to generate a reply to it. Check that the reply message is addressed correctly and send it. Then check that this reply message is also correctly delivered back to you. This is a valuable exercise because it is a further test that you have configured your e-mail client correctly. In particular, it indicates that if other people use *their* reply function to reply to messages they receive from you then those replies will also be correctly addressed and successfully routed to you. It also establishes that any *automatically* generated replies to your messages will reach you. I shall examine the significance of that in the next section.

Return To Sender?

You will probably not be using e-mail for long before you have your first experience of failed e-mail; that is, e-mail which does not get through to the intended recipient for one reason or another.

If you are very unlucky, the message may simply disappear without trace. It has not been delivered, but you receive no indication of this. This is the worst possible situation because you are simply left waiting and wondering. Presumably, at some point, you will assume that the message has not got through, and try sending another message or (better) contacting the person by some other means.

The good news is that this is extremely rare. Internet e-mail is generally very reliable. So while you do not normally receive any explicit indication of *successful* delivery of e-mail, if the attempt to deliver e-mail fails for any reason this almost always generates an explicit error message which is returned to you.

In other words, if you send an e-mail, and do not receive any indication of failure, you are pretty safe to assume that it has been delivered successfully. Mind you, depending on the exact nature of a failure, the report may not come back to you for a few hours or even a few days after you send a message. But for the most common causes of failure, the failure message will be returned to you within minutes.

There is *one* plausible situation where such failure messages may not reach you. Failure messages are, in effect, automatically generated replies to your messages. They are e-mailed back. The address to which they are e-mailed is determined by looking at the original message, specifically the `From:` field included in the header of that message. Provided your e-mail client is configured correctly, this `From:` field will contain your e-mail address, and the failure message will be correctly routed to you. But if this field is not correctly formatted the error messages will never reach you. You can guard against this possibility by going through the procedure detailed at the end of the previous section for checking that replies to your own messages are processed correctly.

Welcome Aboard

What Is This Internet Thing Anyway

Your Net Computer

Getting On-line

The Web

E-mail

Other Internet Services

Welcome Aboard

What Is This Internet Thing Anyway

Your Net Computer

Getting On-line

The Web

E-mail

Other Internet Services

Failure messages normally include some or all of the text of your original message to help you identify it. For this reason messages which fail are said to have been "bounced" by the e-mail system.

When you receive a bounced e-mail message, examine it carefully to try to understand what the nature of the failure is. Unfortunately, there are a great variety of different e-mail handling programs on various Internet e-mail servers. Any given message may have to be routed through several such servers before it reaches its ultimate destination. As a result, there is tremendous variation in the messages returned when e-mail fails. Some of these can be explanatory, but often they are rather obscure.

Far and away the most common reason for e-mail to fail is that the address of one or more recipients has not been entered correctly. Computers are extremely finicky about this. So recheck all the addresses very carefully, character by character.

If you have checked the e-mail addresses carefully, and are sure they are correct, but your message is still getting bounced and you cannot make any further sense of the explanation given in the bounce message, then you should contact the technical support desk of your ISP. You should be able to contact them by e-mail (e.g., in the case of *IOL*, the address is `support@iol.ie`). Forward a copy of the bounce message for them to examine.

Your E-mail Signature

In conventional paper letters, it is normal to put your postal address at the top. This is not strictly necessary in e-mail: your return e-mail address will be included automatically. On the other hand, you may want to provide other contact information - such as your phone number, fax number, and perhaps even postal address (there are still plenty of things that can't be conveniently delivered by e-mail). The Internet e-mail convention is to locate such information at the bottom of your message instead of the top, and it is called a *signature block*, or a *sig* for short.

You could type in your *sig* manually at the bottom of each e-mail message, but it is a good deal more convenient to do it once and then have it copied into new messages automatically. Most e-mail clients support this facility, and MS-OE is no exception. You can find detailed instructions on this by consulting the MS-OE electronic documentation, via the Help menu.

Some people go in for very elaborate signature blocks. For example, personal signatures may include witty or inspirational quotations. In business correspondence you can think of the sig as the equivalent of the letterhead on your business stationery, so you might include a promotional slogan or short advertisement. However, as with quoted text, sigs are most effective when they are used sparingly. As a general rule of thumb, if you use a signature block at all, it should certainly not run to more than four or five lines of text.

An alternative to the simple textual sig described above is to format the signature information in a standardised way as a so-called "virtual card" or *vCard*. The advantage of this is that, by providing contact information in such a standardised format, it makes it easy for a program to extract this information from a received message, and add it to, say, a locally stored electronic address book. Indeed, MS-OE, in conjunction with the Microsoft Address Book (MS-AB) program (which I will discuss further below), does support precisely this sort of automated attachment and extraction of vCard information. On the other hand, this technology is still only gradually gaining support across the Internet, and it is not yet generally safe to assume that recipients will be able to read vCard information.

Textual sigs and vCards are not mutually exclusive of course - you could provide both. For the time being, especially in personal correspondence, I recommend that you settle for a simple textual sig; but if you would like to find out more about vCards, check the Web site for the *Internet Mail Consortium*, the industry organisation responsible for the vCard standard:

http://www.imc.org/

Again, if you want to configure your own vCard with MS-OE, you should consult the electronic documentation, under the Help menu, for detailed instructions.

Getting And Staying Organized

Even if you start off communicating with very few people by e-mail, the common experience is that this circle of e-mail contacts will expand quite rapidly. It is therefore a good idea to give early attention to how you manage your accumulating collection of e-mail before it gets out of hand.

I would recommend that, on an ongoing basis, you consider creating new e-mail folders to collect together correspondence on related subjects. To create a new folder in MS-OE, click on the File menu, then click on Folder, and New Folder... A dialog box appears. It is possible to nest folders within folders, so the dialog box allows you to specify this by clicking on some existing folder to contain the new one. However, initially at least, it is probably enough to have just one level of folders, so click on the top level container (which already contains Inbox etc. immediately below it). You can always reorganise the folder structure later if you wish. Now fill in a name for the new folder and finally click on OK to create the new folder.

Welcome Aboard

What Is This Internet Thing Anyway

Your Net Computer

Getting On-line

The Web

E-mail

Other Internet Services

Welcome
Aboard

What Is This Internet
Thing Anyway

Your Net
Computer

Getting On-line

The Web

E-mail

Other Internet
Services

Now, as you review each new e-mail message you receive, you should immediately decide whether to keep it or delete it. If you want to delete a message then, once it is selected in the Message List, just click on the **Delete** button ☒ in the Tool Bar. If, on the other hand, you decide to keep a message, you should move it out of the Inbox into one of your own folders straight away. You can generally do this just by dragging the message from the Inbox Message List and dropping it into the folder you want to move it to. And of course, if you later want to refile it in a different folder you can again just drag and drop.

By doing this consistently, you can reserve the Inbox folder for holding only new messages that you have not yet reviewed.

Sometimes you may wish to defer deciding about a particular message - for example, you may want to reply to it before filing or deleting it. Even in these cases, I suggest that you immediately move the message from the Inbox folder. You might create a folder called, say, Pending to temporarily hold messages that you are still actively working with.

Another related concern about managing your e-mail correspondence is preserving copies of the messages you yourself send, and filing these along with the relevant correspondence you receive. This is usually quite straightforward because most e-mail clients can be configured to automatically keep a copy of each e-mail message you send. MS-OE is configured to do this by default. These copy messages are placed in the Sent Items folder. To keep your correspondence organised and up to date, you should review and file the messages in this folder (just like the messages in the Inbox folder) each time you send out a batch of e-mail. In this way, the Sent Items folder is reserved to hold only that small collection of outgoing e-mail that you have not yet filed (or deleted).

To Delete Or Undelete?

As already mentioned, when you "delete" messages in MS-OE they are not really immediately deleted. Instead they are moved to a special folder called Deleted Items. Note that this is *not* the same thing as the main Windows 95/98 Recycle Bin, but a separate repository for holding deleted e-mail messages. If you find you have deleted a message in error, you can simply switch to the Deleted Items folder, select the message, and move it back to where you want it.

Of course, because "deleted" messages are not really deleted, but are held in the Deleted Items folder, they are still taking up space on your disk drive. Over time this can build up to be quite a significant amount of wasted storage. I recommend that you empty out the Deleted Items folder, at regular intervals - once every week or couple of weeks. Do this by opening the Deleted Items folder, selecting all messages (click on the Edit menu and then click on Select All), and clicking on the **Delete** button. Alternatively, you can configure MS-OE so that the Deleted Items folder is automatically emptied every time you exit from MS-OE. Do this as follows:

- Open the Options dialog box (click on the Tools menu, then click on Options).

- Click on the Maintenance tab.

- Click on the check box marked:

  Empty messages from the 'Deleted Items' folder on exit.

Note carefully that once a message is deleted from the Deleted Items folder then it is lost and gone forever: it cannot be recovered. So before emptying the folder - either manually, or by exiting MS-OE if automatic emptying has been enabled - be sure that you have not deleted anything you did not intend to!

E-mail Filtering

I have already mentioned the concept of automatic "filtering" of e-mail. The idea is that you can set up one or more criteria that incoming e-mail messages might match; messages matching one or more of those criteria are then automatically processed in some particular way.

Examples of criteria you might use would be that the message was originated by a particular person, or the subject field contains a particular word or phrase. Examples of the sort of action that might be triggered would be to store the message in a particular folder (other than the default folder for incoming e-mail), to generate some kind of automatic response, or to immediately delete the message (unread!).

The most common reason for using filtering is to try to deal with *junk* e-mail. For example, if you find that you are repeatedly getting e-mail from a particular source, that is (from your point of view) junk, you can simply arrange that all e-mail from that source is filtered out and deleted as it arrives. This might seem a bit wasteful: surely it would be better to persuade the individual or organisation responsible for the e-mail to desist from sending it. Unfortunately that often turns out to be an awful lot more trouble than it is worth, and it may be simpler to use a filter.

Filtering for this kind of purpose should be used carefully and sparingly. Otherwise it can easily happen that some messages which you would *not* classify as junk will be automatically deleted, and you may never even realise it has happened.

Welcome Aboard

What Is This Internet Thing Anyway

Your Net Computer

Getting On-line

The Web

E-mail

Other Internet Services

Welcome Aboard

What Is This Internet Thing Anyway

Your Net Computer

Getting On-line

The Web

E-mail

Other Internet Services

Another more general use of filtering is to help with sorting and organising your incoming e-mail. By using suitable filter rules, your incoming e-mail can be automatically sorted into related categories and stored in appropriate folders, even before you look at it. You can then conveniently review new e-mail messages on a related subject at the same time. You may find this preferable to having all incoming e-mail delivered to a single default folder. Using e-mail filters in this way does require some additional discipline in dealing with incoming e-mail. To make sure that you do not overlook important incoming e-mail you should make a habit of regularly checking *all* folders that can automatically receive new messages.

In general MS-OE allows at least the basic filtering of e-mail messages into specific folders, and may also support more complex actions such as generating automatic replies, or automatically forwarding a message to other addresses. The details do vary significantly depending on the particular version of the program which you are using, so you should use the following discussion only as a general guide to the principles involved. Definitive instructions for any particular version of MS-OE, or any other e-mail client, will generally be available in its electronic documentation (i.e., under the Help menu for the program).

MS-OE filtering is set up or configured by defining a list of individual message filtering *rules*, which will be applied in sequence to each message as it is received. Each filtering rule consists of one or more *conditions* together with one or more *actions*.

The conditions potentially include such criteria as:

- Whether particular words or phrases appear in any of the To:, From:, Cc: or Subject: header fields, or anywhere in the body of a message.

- Which e-mail account the message was delivered to (this is only relevant if you have configured multiple e-mail accounts into MS-OE).

- Whether the message size exceeds a given threshold.

- Whether the message has any *attachments*. Attachments are separate computer files included along with a conventional, textual, e-mail message. This is a topic in its own right, and I will return to it in detail further below.

If you specify multiple criteria in a single rule, then you will also have to specify whether they must *all* be matched by a given message, or whether it is sufficient if *any one* of them is matched, in order for the specified action(s) to be taken.

Potential actions include:

- To move or copy the message to a folder. Copying preserves a copy in its "original" destination folder, whereas moving does not.

- To delete the message - though this is really just a more specific case of moving it (i.e., moving it to the `Deleted Items` folder).

- To forward the message to one or more other e-mail address.

- To reply automatically with some previously prepared message. A common application of this is a so-called "vacation" message, which you might set up before going away on holiday, just to warn people that you will not be checking you e-mail for a while. Of course, in that particular case, this must be combined with configuring `MS-OE` to automatically go online and check for new e-mail, say once a day or so. Again, check the electronic documentation for details.

As far as possible, you should always *test* any new filtering rule by composing a message of your own, designed to match the criteria, and e-mailing it to yourself. Verify that, on receipt, it gets filtered as you expected. You can easily test rules involving the contents of the `Subject:` field in this way. You can also test rules using the `To:` and `Cc:` fields, though that will also generally involve sending the test message to people other than yourself, so you should try to minimise this. It is more difficult to test rules based on the `From:` field, even though these may be the most useful. If possible, when you introduce such rules you should contact the relevant person and request them to send you a test message. Otherwise, I simply recommend that, after establishing a new filter based on the `From:` field, you should be especially vigilant to ensure that it is not behaving in some unexpected manner.

You can define as many filter rules as you like in `MS-OE`. However, be careful to note that they may interact in unexpected ways. In particular, it may be possible for a given message to match more than one filter rule. The outcome may then not be what you had intended. `MS-OE` applies rules strictly in the order in which they appear in the rules dialog box: whichever is the *first* one to match a given message will be the *only* one to be applied to that message. If necessary, you can use the **Move Up** and **Move Down** buttons on this dialog box to move a given rule up or down, and thus change the order in which they are tested. You can also specify, as an action for a particular rule, that no further rules should be processed.

My general advice would be to think hard before introducing any e-mail filtering rules. Be sure that any prospective rule will apply to a sufficient volume of messages to justify the unexpected problems which it may give rise to. Keep your rules as simple as possible. Do not introduce too many rules. Introduce new rules strictly one

Welcome Aboard

What Is This Internet Thing Anyway

Your Net Computer

Getting On-line

The Web

E-mail

Other Internet Services

Welcome Aboard

What Is This Internet Thing Anyway

Your Net Computer

Getting On-line

The Web

E-mail

Other Internet Services

at a time. Explicitly test new rules if that is at all possible. If not, then each time you add a new rule, wait for a while to see whether it is behaving as you expected before adding more. Provided you follow these guidelines, e-mail filtering rules can be a very useful and beneficial tool in managing your e-mail.

Using An Electronic Address Book

As you continue to use e-mail, you will build up a list of e-mail addresses of friends and associates that you communicate with. You can, of course, maintain this list of contacts in the traditional way in a paper address book. However, since you will most usually collect e-mail addresses from your computer, and will want to use them on your computer, it will be convenient to use the computer itself to store and manage the address book in electronic form.

There are stand-alone software packages for handling this kind of job. Alternatively, most e-mail clients will also have some kind of address book facility built into them. Either way, your address book program should be integrated with your e-mail client so that you can easily move relevant information between them.

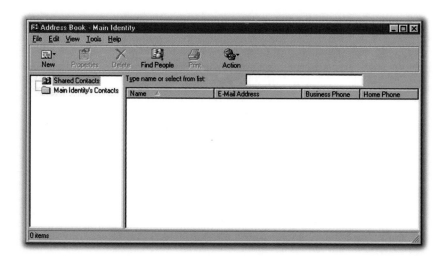

I will look briefly at the Microsoft *Windows Address Book* or MS-AB (also sometimes referred to as *Internet Explorer Address Book*). This is a stand-alone package, but is included in the MS-IE suite of programs. It is well integrated with MS-IE and MS-OE. Other address book packages will offer very similar facilities.

If you are already running MS-OE (or, indeed, MS-IE) you can invoke MS-AB directly from the Tool Bar. Alternatively, you should be able to start it directly via the **Start** button (look under Internet Explorer or Accessories).

The general layout of the main MS-AB window should now look quite familiar, with Title, Menu, Tool and Status Bars. The main part of the window is taken up with the *contact* list. This will list all the contacts you have inserted in the address book.

To add a contact, click on the New button and then on New Contact. This will give a Properties dialog box, in which you can enter information about this particular person. You can generally fill in as much or as little information as you want, though, as a very minimum, you must provide a name (at least one of First, Middle or Last name). We are discussing the address book in the context of keeping track of e-mail addresses, so presumably you will also enter an e-mail address. However, if you want, you can use MS-AB to keep track of *all* the people and organisations you regularly communicate with, not just those with e-mail access, so you *can* leave that field blank if you wish.

Click on the various tabs on the Properties dialog box to see what other information you might optionally add to the address box. Most of them are self-explanatory, but if you need more explanation, use the **Help** button **?** in the dialog box Title Bar to get more information on any particular field.

Once you have added some new contacts in this way, they will appear in the contact list in the main MS-AB window. If you want to change the information for any contact, just select that line in the list and click in the Properties button, and the Properties dialog box will reappear.

The contact list is normally displayed in alphabetical order. With a short list it is easy to find any name you want, but as you build up a more extensive contact list, this will become a little harder. At this stage it is convenient to start typing the name you want into the field above the message list. As you type, the address list will be restricted to just those contacts matching what you have typed.

To start creating an e-mail message to a particular person, from MS-AB, follow these steps:

* Click on the person's entry in the contact list.

* Click on the Action button in the Tool Bar.

* Click on Send Mail.

An MS-OE e-mail composition window will then appear, addressed to that person.

Welcome Aboard

What Is This Internet Thing Anyway

Your Net Computer

Getting On-line

The Web

E-mail

Other Internet Services

Welcome Aboard

What Is This Internet Thing Anyway

Your Net Computer

Getting On-line

The Web

E-mail

Other Internet Services

Conversely, if you are operating from within MS-OE you can access the address book, as necessary. I have already mentioned that you can start up MS-AB via the Tool Bar of MS-OE. Additionally, whenever you have an e-mail composition window you can choose recipients directly from the address book. Click on the Tools menu of the composition window and then click on Select Recipients. This will bring up a Select Recipients dialog box, again listing all contacts from the address book, and allowing you to select people to be added to the To:, Cc: or Bcc: fields of the new message. The dialog is fairly self-explanatory, but, as usual, there is a **Help** button **?** in the dialog box Title Bar.

A common address book activity is to add new contacts that you have received e-mail from. If you are reading a newly received message in the viewing pane of the MS-OE main window, follow these steps to create a new address book entry for the recipient:

- Double click on the message in the message list. This will create a separate window displaying this message.

- Click on the Tools menu in the window.

- Click on Add To Address Book.

- A submenu appears, showing all the people addressed by this message. Click on the one you want to add to the address book.

- An MS-AB Properties dialog box will now appear with information extracted from the header of the e-mail message already filled in. Minimally, this will include the e-mail address. You can now manually fill in additional information if you wish.

- Click on OK in the Properties dialog, and the new contact will be inserted in the address book.

As previously mentioned, if an e-mail message has an attached vCard you can also extract that to add the information to MS-AB - see the online help for more detailed information on this.

The final MS-AB facility worth mentioning here is the ability to set up "groups" or "lists" of contacts that you copy e-mail to at the same time. I mentioned earlier how the ability to address many people is a key advantage of e-mail over conventional paper post. If there are groups of people you regularly want to send e-mail to - such as members of a club or committee - then it is convenient to organise their e-mail addresses under a single common "group" name. Then, whenever you want to send an e-mail to all of them, you need only address it to the "group name" and everyone in the group will receive a copy.

To establish such a group in MS-AB, follow these steps:

- Click on the New button, and then on New Group. A Properties dialog box will appear for the group.

- Click in the Group Name field in this dialog box, and enter some convenient name for the new group.

- Click on the Select Members button. A Select Group Members dialog box will appear.

- Click on a contact to add to the group.

- Click on the Select button.

- Repeat this selection for each person you want in the group.

- Click on OK to dismiss the Select Group Members dialog box.

- Click on OK on the group Properties dialog box. The group will then appear in your contact list, along with your individual contacts.

Now, whenever you want to send an e-mail message to all the members of this group, follow the same procedure used for choosing recipients from the address book from within an e-mail composition window: click on the Tools menu of the composition window, and then click on Select Recipients, except now you'll be able to choose the whole group in one go, under the group name. It's as simple as that!

The Importance Of Being Backed Up

Over time, as you build up an archive of e-mail correspondence, whether personal, business, or both, and a personal address book of e-mail contacts, you will be making a very substantial investment of time, energy, and money. E-mail materials will probably not be the *only* valuable information stored on your computer, but discussing e-mail certainly gives us a good context to briefly mention the general subject of protecting your investments in electronic information.

Given how complex modern personal computers are, they are remarkably reliable. Nonetheless, they are *not* perfect, and they do occasionally break down. Sometimes when this happens some or all of the data stored on them is *irretrievably* lost. It is never too soon to start taking precautions against this! You can protect yourself against a disastrous failure of your computer by "backing up" the data - copying it onto some external medium. All PCs these days are equipped with diskette drives and these can be used for backups. However, as the volume of data stored continues to grow, the number of diskettes, and time, required to make a backup can quickly

Welcome Aboard

What Is This Internet Thing Anyway

Your Net Computer

Getting On-line

The Web

E-mail

Other Internet Services

Welcome Aboard

What Is This Internet Thing Anyway

Your Net Computer

Getting On-line

The Web

E-mail

Other Internet Services

become prohibitive. Better alternatives would be to fit your PC with a high capacity tape drive or removable media disk drive.

I recommend that you establish a habit of backing up the information on your computer about once a week. Since this normally only involves backing up those files which have actually changed in that period (a so-called "incremental" backup), the weekly routine need not be onerous.

More detailed procedures for backing up (or restoring) the data on your computer are beyond the scope of this book. However, if you look up the topic *backup* in the Windows electronic help system you will find further information.

Smile—You're On E-mail!

Written communication has always suffered in comparison to face-to-face conversation in that the participants cannot directly gauge each other's responses. You cannot see the other person smiling, or frowning, or thumping the table, or backing away. This lack of the normal cues of "body language" sometimes means that written communications can be badly misunderstood.

This problem has become a lot worse with e-mail. E-mail is very immediate: one can receive and respond (irrevocably) to e-mail in seconds. With paper post, one at least had the time it takes to walk to the postbox to reconsider, and perhaps decide that a response was a little too strong or emotional. Furthermore, the global nature of the Internet makes it much more common that we exchange e-mail with people whom we have never met, who may have very different cultural values, and whose native language may well be different from our own. The possibilities for talking at cross purposes are greatly increased.

Fortunately, some useful conventions have grown up to help cope with this. These do not solve all the problems, but they certainly cut down on *some* of the confusions that e-mail exchanges can otherwise lead to.

Firstly, and as a crude generalisation, e-mail correspondence has evolved a much lighter, less formal style than traditional business writing. Even e-mail used for business purposes tends to be a lot more like a personal letter.

Secondly, and more importantly, ways have been invented to reinsert into written communication some of the emphasis and rhythm that is present in natural speech, and some of the non-verbal body language that we use when face to face, particularly smiles and frowns, but also more nebulous gestures such as nods or winks.

Emphasis is usually shown in typeset text using *italics* or perhaps **boldface** type. As I have explained, you cannot generally rely on such attributes being correctly preserved in e-mail. Instead we usually use CAPITALS (also interpreted as SHOUT-ING), or *emphasise* text using the asterisk (*) character. Underlining can also be suggested by surrounding a word with the _underscore_ character.

As for non-verbal signals, in the simplest case they can be conveyed just by inserting an extra tell-tale word or phrase at an appropriate place, somewhat like stage directions in a script:

```
... I would love to go to her party, except I think
I'm washing my hair that night [wink]...

That's great news - I'm delighted [GRIN]...

I *really* don't think that is such a great idea
[paternal frown]...

Well, you must do as you think best dear, it's none
of *my* business <shrug>...
```

This idea of inserting non-verbal gestures or expressions into e-mail messages has also led to the idea of what are called *emoticons* or *smileys*. These are little "letter pictures" or icons made up of ordinary textual characters, which - with a little imagination - can be seen as representing facial expressions. While dozens of these have been suggested, there are only a few that are widely used (and recognised). You will probably find these easier to recognise if you tilt your head sideways, to the left:

> :-) The original "smiley face". Indicates humor, friendliness, and sometimes sarcasm. A simpler form with no "nose" is also often used :)

> :-(The classic "frowny face"', for sadness, anger, disapproval etc.

> ;-) The "half-smiley" or "winky", indicating that a statement is not meant to be taken too seriously.

Just as in face-to-face communication, overuse of any gesture or expression will quickly become boring, if not positively annoying, to the listener/reader. So use smileys lightly and appropriately, and don't get carried away.

Fatal Attachment?

So far I have discussed e-mail strictly in terms of exchanging textual messages. This is tremendously useful, and accounts for the vast majority of e-mail activity. However, the e-mail facility can actually support much more sophisticated messaging, which I will briefly discuss here - not least because along with this extra sophistication comes extra danger!

Welcome Aboard

What Is This Internet Thing Anyway

Your Net Computer

Getting On-line

The Web

E-mail

Other Internet Services

Welcome Aboard

What Is This Internet Thing Anyway

Your Net Computer

Getting On-line

The Web

E-mail

Other Internet Services

The essential idea is that it is possible to "attach" any kind of information at all (that you have in computer form) to an e-mail message; the recipient can then detach it again and view or process it in whatever way is appropriate. The buzzword acronym for this facility is *MIME*, for Multipurpose Internet Mail Extensions. With MIME attachments you can use e-mail to send photographs, songs, movies, or any other kind of information you can imagine. Of course, you must separately have some way of getting these media into your computer - but that may be easier than you might expect. A multimedia PC will normally already have a facility for you to record sound into a computer file. If you have a scanner or a digital camera you can easily create image files. And so on.

Naturally, you can also use MIME attachments to exchange more conventional computer information - such as spreadsheet files, databases, word processor files, or even applications programs. This can be *much* more convenient that exchanging information with others using diskettes (which is the more old-fashioned way of doing things).

Using attachments is a relatively advanced facility, and I won't present it in detail here - you can find more information in the documentation for your e-mail client. But I do want to warn you about one *danger* of e-mail attachments: the real possibility it raises of efficiently transmitting computer *viruses*.

Computer viruses, unlike their real biological counterparts, are not natural occurrences: they are carefully crafted weapons of computer terrorism. A virus is a malicious computer program that can "infect", or become installed on, your computer, without your being aware of it. It can then cause various kinds of malfunction, ranging from the mildly annoying through to wholesale destruction of your computer data. It can also use your computer as a base to propagate to others.

The most common mechanism which viruses have used to spread themselves in the past is via floppy disks shared between computer users. However - and this is the what I want to alert you to here - they *can* propagate equally, or perhaps ever better, via e-mail.

A well-publicised incident of this sort was that of the so-called *Melissa* virus. This exists embedded within documents in the *Microsoft Word* (a word processing program) format. To a certain extent, Melissa can be passed on just "naturally", whenever people exchange infected documents (whether by e-mail or on disk). But the specially distinctive feature of Melissa is that it does not passively wait and hope for propagation in this way: once it gets to infect your machine it can not only replicate itself into *your* documents (which is a common technique that many viruses of this sort use) it also actively scans your e-mail address book, and sends e-mails, with infected documents attached, to a large number of your e-mail contacts. Because these e-mails *appear* to be coming from you, there is a good chance that the recipients may believe that the attachment is trustworthy. If so, they will duly detach it and load it up in MS-Word - at which point it gets an opportunity to infect *their* systems also. And so the cycle repeats, but multiplying rapidly.

Melissa was not designed to do any "direct" damage to users' computers or data as such - though in certain circumstances it could transmit documents, belonging to a victim, which were sensitive or confidential. But when it was initially released, in late March 1999, it spread extremely quickly on a global scale. The resulting explosion in e-mail traffic quickly overloaded many e-mail servers in affected organisations, severely disrupting their normal operations.

While the Melissa virus itself has now been generally brought under control, new viruses are regularly being released. So you would be very wise to take precautions against them. The minimal precaution against viruses of all sorts is to install effective anti-virus software on your computer. However, in general these can only fully protect you against viruses that have already been detected and analysed (or close variants of such viruses) . So you should also be extremely careful about exposing your computer to infection in the first place.

As far as protecting yourself against infection (and transmission) of viruses by *e-mail* is concerned, the simplest policy, which I certainly recommend for beginners, is to confine yourself strictly to plain text (ASCII) format messages, with no attachments. This form of e-mail is absolutely safe: it is impossible for viruses to hide in such messages. In particular, you should resist the temptation to use a sophisticated word processor, such as MS-Word, to create straightforward textual messages which can be dealt with perfectly adequately in ASCII. This is a trap that many novice Internet users fall into, especially if they are already familiar with using a word processing package. Similarly, If you find that any of your e-mail correspondents is in the habit of using such a word processor format for textual messages, warn them about the danger of propagating viruses, and encourage them to use ASCII instead.

More generally, if you receive e-mail with attachments of any format then, regardless of who the message is apparently from, do not attempt to access or view these attachments unless you can independently verify their authenticity and purpose, and that the sender has taken steps to ensure that they are virus-free.

There are many Web sites which provide information on computer viruses and other issues relating to computer security. A good starting point is the following Google directory:

```
http://directory.google.com/Top/Computers/Security/
```

Welcome Aboard

What Is This Internet Thing Anyway

Your Net Computer

Getting On-line

The Web

E-mail

Other Internet Services

Welcome Aboard

What Is This Internet Thing Anyway

Your Net Computer

Getting On-line

The Web

E-mail

Other Internet Services

As the name "virus" indicates, some of the ideas behind the design of computer viruses have an inspiration from biological agents. However, alongside this malicious *application* of certain biological ideas, there are also completely *positive* research programs dealing with related concepts and technology. One such field, explicitly concerned with the intersection between biology, engineering, and computer science has become known as "Artificial Life" or *ALife*. You can find out more about this benign face of biologically inspired computer programming at:

```
http://www.eeng.dcu.ie/~alife/
```

Reprise: Web-based e-mail...

Although the detail of this chapter has been based on the idea of using a local e-mail client program, such as MS–OE, I also mentioned earlier the possibility of accessing your e-mail through the Web instead. While this has the obvious disadvantage that you must be online, and thus potentially incurring call charges, while you do it, it can also have some significant advantages. Firstly, it offers *mobile* or *roving* access to your e-mail; so that, for example, you can easily check your e-mail both at home and at work or college, or when you are away on a trip - anywhere, in fact, that you can use a Web browser (e.g., at an Internet Cafe or Kiosk). Closely related to this, Web-based e-mail allows access using devices that may not have the hardware or software capability to handle e-mail offline - such as Net TV units, or Internet enabled video game consoles. A final possible attraction is that by using one of these services you can separate your e-mail address from your Internet *connection* service - allowing you to retain the same e-mail address even if you switch to using a different ISP for your connection service, for whatever reason.

Many organisations offer Web-based e-mail services. And, in the case of *IOL*, for example, you can have the best of both worlds - because the same e-mail account or mailbox can be accessed either through a Web interface or through a local client program, whichever is more convenient at any given time!

In any case, all the general principles of e-mail discussed in this chapter, such as replying and forwarding, the use of folders and an address book, attachments and so on, are all equally applicable regardless of which sort of interface is used.

And In Conclusion...

Well, there it is, the magic - and the dangers - of Internet e-mail. I hope that, like me, you find that it opens up a whole new world of people to communicate with, from close at home to far away. Have fun, and keep smiling ;-)

6. Other Internet Services

I n the previous two chapters you have read about the two core services that every Internet user should master: the World Wide Web and personal e-mail. But there are many other services available on the Internet - indeed, new ones are being introduced all the time. In this final chapter I will briefly review a selection of these other services. Some are completely separate from the core e-mail and Web services, others overlap heavily with them. In each case I will describe the general idea behind the service and give some pointers on where to find more detailed information.

E-commerce?

But first, another buzzword, and one that is very much the current flavour: "electronic commerce" or *e-commerce*. So what is it?

E-commerce is not a separate, distinct, service available through the Internet - rather it is just a general name for *any* kind of transaction, where money changes hands, that is carried out using the Internet. Most commonly, it refers to a service of some sort that is accessed via your Web browser, but it can equally apply to something involving e-mail, or any of the other more specialised Internet services that will be discussed below.

The hype and excitement about e-commerce reflects the fact that many businesses believe that this is the way of the future. In particular, they feel that many goods and services that are currently traded by "conventional" means - shops, wholesalers, agents, brokers etc. - could be traded equally well, or perhaps even better, by using the Internet. Of course, this becomes a genuinely feasible alternative only when a sufficient number of people and businesses are in a position to access the Internet. But it seems likely that this sort of break-through level of access may already have been reached in some countries (especially the USA) and will certainly arrive very soon in many others - such as Ireland. As a result, many organisations are struggling to anticipate what the impact will be on their own ways of doing business; and are at least experimenting with some form of online business or e-commerce.

Welcome Aboard

What Is This Internet Thing Anyway

Your Net Computer

Getting On-line

The Web

E-mail

Other Internet Services

Welcome Aboard

What Is This Internet Thing Anyway

Your Net Computer

Getting On-line

The Web

E-mail

Other Internet Services

It is already possible to engage in many commercial activities using the Internet. Here's a small sample:

- Booking airline tickets.

- Making hotel reservations.

- Managing your bank accounts.

- Buying books.

- Tracking courier deliveries.

... and this is just the tip of the iceberg!

Of course, a common factor in almost everything that can be described as e-commerce is the need to be able to exchange money - to buy and sell in an online environment. At the moment this is generally done by using credit cards. You may be concerned about passing on your credit card details over the Internet, in case they may be intercepted or otherwise abused. Some caution is certainly appropriate. Reputable e-commerce sites will operate a so-called "secure" server which encrypts or disguises any sensitive information as it is transmitted - thus making them a good deal less vulnerable to eavesdropping that say, conventional phone or FAX communications. But that, in itself, does not guarantee that the business you are dealing with is trustworthy. So, as a general rule, if you are going to use the Internet for electronic transactions of any sort, you should exercise the same care that would be appropriate to any other kind of business dealing. You should ensure, as far as possible, that you are dealing with established, reputable organisations. Ideally, look for recommendations from people you know and trust.

While credit cards are commonly used to support e-commerce today, this is a rather clumsy and awkward system - especially for small value and one-off transactions. Furthermore, in using a credit card, you automatically surrender some degree of privacy (compared to using cash). The solution to this will be some sort of "electronic" cash. This technology is still only at the development stage, but the pent-up demand for it is now so great that we can expect a de facto standard to emerge and be widely deployed in the foreseeable future. This will dramatically expand the opportunities for high quality, profitable, commerce on the Web. This will not displace the existing, free Internet services, but it will greatly enhance the range and quality of services which can be accessed. So we can look forward to the emergence of new, and perhaps unimagined, services via the Internet for quite some time to come!

But now, let's return to looking at more of the variety of *existing* Internet services - both old and new.

Telnet

Telnet, along with FTP (see below) and e-mail, was one of the original services offered on the early Internet. It is still widely used, although much of its functionality is progressively being taken over by the World Wide Web.

To understand Telnet we have to think back to an earlier era of computer technology, when computer power was much more expensive than today. Then it was typical for a company or organisation to have a single large ("mainframe") computer for all its computer requirements. Individual users did not have their own desktop computers. Instead they had much more basic and low-cost devices called computer *terminals*. These were directly wired to the mainframe. A terminal had a monitor and keyboard, but was "dumb": it just relayed keystrokes to the mainframe computer, and displayed its responses, it could not do any computing of its own. Most terminals could display only monochrome text, no colour, no graphic images and no sound (apart from the occasional "beep").

Nonetheless, users could run a wide variety of applications on the mainframe computers - accounting, stock control, reservation systems, library catalogues and so on. Sometimes they even handled wordprocessing, spreadsheets and e-mail.

Although computer technology has now moved on a long way, these older systems have not disappeared. For some applications this centralised approach is still technically the most effective. In others, while it might not be the *most* effective approach, it is still perfectly satisfactory and the costs of replacing the system with completely new technology are prohibitive.

When personal computers first started to become available they were deployed side by side with the old terminals. Users would switch between the terminal and the PC depending on what they needed to do. It was quickly noticed that since much the same hardware was present in both machines (keyboard and monitor), it should be possible for the same machine to do both jobs. And indeed it is! At first this was done by directly wiring the PC to the mainframe, in the same way that the terminal had previously been wired. By running a suitable "terminal emulation" program on the PC, it could emulate or imitate the operation of the terminal. Later on, as PCs were networked together, it became more convenient to also wire the mainframe computers to this same network, rather than use the separate dedicated type of wiring required by the dumb terminals.

This trend is brought to its logical conclusion with the Internet and *Telnet:* any PC connected to the Internet, and running a Telnet client program, can interact with any mainframe computer connected to the Internet that is running a Telnet server program. The net effect is that you can make your local personal computer pretend

Welcome Aboard

What Is This Internet Thing Anyway

Your Net Computer

Getting On-line

The Web

E-mail

Other Internet Services

Welcome Aboard

What Is This Internet Thing Anyway

Your Net Computer

Getting On-line

The Web

E-mail

Other Internet Services

to be a dumb terminal directly connected to a mainframe - even though that mainframe may be on the opposite side of the world. This turns out to be a surprisingly flexible and useful thing to be able to do!

Telnet servers on the Internet divide into two general kinds: private and public.

Private servers are essentially the same mainframes as of old. They are operating dedicated software for the particular needs of some company or organisation. To access one of these machines you need to be duly authorised, and have been issued with a specific username and password. Typically this mechanism is used by employees to access systems on their organisations' private computers when they are working from some remote location. A growing application is for people "tele-working" from home, either full or part time. The system allows the employee to use a dialup Internet connection to access services that previously would have required some kind of dedicated or special purpose connection to the computer site. Another useful application is for Web-site administrators to be able to remotely update and maintain their systems.

Public servers, on the other hand, are specifically intended to be available to anyone on the Internet. A wide range of services is available in this way, from airline reservations to playing multi-user games (which I will return to later).

Many of these services are beginning to provide access through Web Browsers as an alternative to Telnet - offering richer multimedia capabilities. But that is a long-term process. In the meantime, Telnet is still very convenient.

As to the mechanics of using Telnet, you will need a Telnet client program. One is included with Windows, as the program `telnet.exe` in the `windows` folder. You can start it up manually like this:

- Click on the `Start` button in the task bar.
- Click on `Run`.
- Type in `Telnet` and click on `OK`.
- Click on the `Connect` menu item.
- Click on `Remote System`. The `Connect` dialog box appears.
- Enter a `Host` Name (the Internet name of the remote server computer you wish to connect to).
- Click on `Connect`. The connection should then be established. If required, you will be prompted for a username and password to log in.

Alternatively, you can start Telnet and specify the remote server at the same time by entering or following a `telnet` URL in your Web Browser.

In either case, once the Telnet client is running, you can use the `Help` menu to get additional information.

File Transfer Protocol: FTP

I mentioned FTP previously in discussing the history of the Internet. It is the name both of a protocol, or set of rules, for exchanging files between Internet computers, and for client and server programs that understand this protocol. As with Telnet, FTP was one of the original Internet services, but is now becoming less important. The FTP protocol is being displaced, for many purposes, by the more sophisticated HTTP (Hypertext Transfer Protocol). Also, since Web Browsers can act as clients for both HTTP and FTP, specific FTP client programs are not as necessary as they used to be.

However, there are a couple of situations where FTP clients are still useful. Firstly, when downloading particularly large files from the Internet, it is sometimes more efficient (faster) and more reliable to do it via FTP, and using a dedicated FTP client, than by using a Web browser.

Secondly, using an FTP client allows you to *upload* files to remote machines. Most Web Browsers and HTTP servers do not yet support this very well. This might be particularly useful if your ISP allows you to put your own files on a Web server, for others to browse (see the next section). You can prepare and maintain the materials on your own computer, using FTP to upload revised versions to the ISP's Web server when necessary.

Windows does include a very basic FTP client. You can start it up via the `Start` button, as described above for Telnet, but entering `ftp` as the command name. However, there is no proper electronic help, and use of the program relies on a rather cryptic set of commands. I do not recommend this program for beginners. Both of the following sites provide better alternative FTP client programmes for Windows:

```
http://www.cuteftp.com/
```

```
http://www.wsftp.com/
```

Note that software distributed over the Internet will be either "freeware" or "shareware". Freeware is free of charge. Shareware is not. You are allowed to download and try out Shareware programs for a specified period (typically 30 days). If you want to continue using the software after that you must register it by sending payment to the publisher. Registration may bring additional benefits such as a printed manual, support, and a higher functionality version of the program.

Welcome Aboard

What Is This Internet Thing Anyway

Your Net Computer

Getting On-line

The Web

E-mail

Other Internet Services

Welcome Aboard

What Is This Internet Thing Anyway

Your Net Computer

Getting On-line

The Web

E-mail

Other Internet Services

Build Your Own Web Site

Most ISPs include an allocation of "web space" as part of their standard service, meaning that you are permitted to upload materials of your own onto a Web server operated by that ISP. Those materials will then be accessible to anyone, anywhere else on the world, who chooses to do so. For example, the *IOL Free* service includes 10MByte of such space, while *IOL Gold* offers 100MByte.

Why would you want to do such a thing?

Well, you might do it just for fun. It's a bit like operating an "amateur radio" station - you may make contact with people around the world with similar interests. You might put your CV on the Web, as a way of promoting yourself to potential employers. You might use a Web site to highlight some cause or organisation you are involved with. You might help a local school to establish a Web presence, and use it to link up with other schools in Ireland or elsewhere. A club you belong might use a Web site to promote its activities, communicate with existing members and attract new ones.

Unfortunately the mechanics of establishing and maintaining a Web presence are quite technical, and the details are well beyond our scope here. But I can give you a few starting points.

First, it is very important to spend at least a few months becoming familiar with the Web before you even think about a Web site of your own. Make a note of sites that you like. You can use these both as places to provide links to from your own pages, and also as guidelines for design.

There are two aspects to any Web site: appearance and content. Appearance is simply the style of the site - whether it has images, forms, music and so on. Content is the actual information or service provided by the site. Appearance is important; but content is king. Furthermore, Web pages with a complex appearance are correspondingly complicated to design and implement, and are best left to professional graphic designers. For home-brew web sites I recommend that you keep the style simple, and concentrate on offering useful content that visitors will value.

Check the exact conditions attaching to the availability of Web space from your ISP. For example, with *IOL*, you must agree to abide by an *Acceptable Usage Policy* in respect of materials you might load in your Web space. You can review this policy at:

```
http://register.iol.ie/webspace/
```

You will see that the conditions are not onerous, basically just ensuring that you operate your personal Web site in a legal and responsible manner. Note that *IOL* does not impose any restrictions on the use of personal Web space for "commercial" purposes - which is not necessarily true of all ISPs.

Basic Web pages must be prepared in the HTML format. There are many tools available which will help with this. For example, the Netscape Communicator suite of programs includes a HTML editor called *Netscape Composer*, and the *Microsoft Office 2000* suite provides a wide range of tools for Web site development. *IOL* provides a guide to setting up your own Web site, at:

> http://help.iolfree.ie/websites/

You can generally test Web materials locally before you load them on to your ISP's server. That is, your Browser should be able to open local files stored on your hard disk, and follow links between them. Do as much of this kind of testing as possible so that visitors to your pages will not encounter problems.

Be careful of the fact that HTML pages can appear significantly different depending on what Browser is used to view them. Just because a page looks well with your Browser, with your normal settings, does not mean it will look as well for others. I recommend that you at least test your pages with both Netscape Navigator and Microsoft Internet Explorer; and that, for each Browser, you try a variety of different Window sizes and shapes. Also remember that some people will choose not to download embedded images at all (because downloading is too slow, or perhaps the person has a visual impairment which means they cannot see the images anyway).

Once you upload your materials to the ISP site, test these "live" versions again. In particular, make sure that any links from your pages to other locations on the Web are working as you expected. If possible, ask friends to check the appearance of the pages as well - particularly if they will be accessing them with different Browsers, or from far distant locations, both of which may affect the perceived quality of your site. Maintain your pages. Make a regular check that links from your pages are still operational, and that information you give has not gone out of date: for example a banner headline announcing an "upcoming" event, that actually happened six months ago. Such discrepancies give a very poor impression to the visitor.

For further excellent advice on Web site engineering, try these sites:

> http://www.useit.com

> http://www.arsdigita.com

Welcome Aboard

What Is This Internet Thing Anyway

Your Net Computer

Getting On-line

The Web

E-mail

Other Internet Services

Welcome Aboard

What Is This Internet Thing Anyway

Your Net Computer

Getting On-line

The Web

E-mail

Other Internet Services

Web Portals

Web "portals" have become very popular in recent years. The idea of a portal site is that a particular provider draws together and integrates a variety of services, that might previously have been operated on separate sites by independent providers. The big potential advantage for users is that you can gain access to this variety of services in a consistent way, with a single "look and feel" for your interactions with the services. In this way a portal can significantly simplify use of the Internet - and allow you to concentrate on getting the information and services you want rather than learning how to navigate around yet another uniquely structured and designed site. Note that, in general, a portal provider will not necessarily actually operate all the services it provides access to; rather, it may just provide a standardised "front end" or interface to a service that is largely provided by another operator.

An excellent example of a portal site is that provided by *IOL* whichI have already mentioned earlier:

```
http://www.iol.ie/
```

This single site provides integrated access to wide variety of services, including:

- News and Weather
- E-mail, free SMS, chat and instant messanger
- Travel
- Sport
- Shopping
- Leisure/Entertainment
- Access to the *Google* powered search engine with unique Ireland only search and directories.

It is particularly convenient to set up a portal site, such as this, as your *Home* page (accessed from your browser's Home button).

Multi-user Services

Despite all the hype, the Internet is essentially just a medium for human communication. Its importance is not in the technicality of the computers and the networks, but in the novel forms of human communication it supports. So far, I have discussed two of these forms of communication in detail, the Web and e-mail. Both of these can be viewed as electronic variations on traditional forms of non-electronic communication:

- E-mail is inspired by the idea of paper correspondence: communication from single authors to single recipients. I call this *One-To-One* Communication.

- The Web is tailored for *publishing*: the communication of information from any single author to indefinitely many recipients. This is largely a one way process, and I call it *One-To-Many* communication.

This points - by omission - at another very common form of human communication: *Many-To-Many*. In the computer world, this is also referred to by the term *Multi-user* service or system.

A typical example of conventional Many-To-Many communication would be something like a meeting, conference or seminar. There are a number of participants, and, in principle, each can simultaneously communicate with any or all of the others. Many-To-Many communication also describes many social activities with more formal rules that we normally regard as *entertainment* - board games, quiz competitions and so on.

Traditional Many-To-Many communication is strongly constrained by simple practical considerations. It only works at all provided the number of participants is kept fairly small. The participants generally need to be in the same physical location at the same time. Some rules or protocols (perhaps controlled through a "chairman") may be required to ensure different people get a chance to speak, that no single person monopolises the discussion, that the group remains focussed on the topic at hand, and (most importantly) that the meeting ends on time. And if the meeting is to have some long term benefit, it might be useful if someone keeps some record of the proceedings so that minutes, or even verbatim transcripts, can be preserved and circulated.

Not surprisingly, a number of attempts have been made to use networked computers - and the Internet in particular - to deliver some corresponding kind of Many-To-Many communication, or multi-user service. The state of the art here is very dynamic: we must be satisfied with a brief survey.

Newsgroups, Mailing Lists And All That...

The longest established approaches to Multi-user electronic communication have grown out of the basic idea of the e-mail service. These systems are based on electronic *pooling* of textual messages among some groups of people.

Welcome Aboard

What Is This Internet Thing Anyway

Your Net Computer

Getting On-line

The Web

E-mail

Other Internet Services

Welcome Aboard

What Is This Internet Thing Anyway

Your Net Computer

Getting On-line

The Web

E-mail

Other Internet Services

I have already introduced this idea in Chapter **5**, when discussing the idea of e-mail "groups" in MS–OE. We saw there that you could create a list of e-mail addresses as a "group", and then send copies of e-mail to the whole group as easily as to any single person.

Well now suppose that everyone in the group *also* has a copy of that same group list. Then everyone can both post messages to the whole group and receive all messages posted to the group by everyone else. In effect, such a shared group or mailing list establishes the possibility of an ongoing conversation or discussion among all the members, just like a conventional meeting or conference.

Unlike an ordinary meeting, this particular kind of electronic conference does not happen in any fixed place or time. The participants can be distributed all over the globe. The conference need not start or stop at particular times. Any given participant can choose when to review new messages that have been contributed to the discussion. He or she can then make additional contributions, and promptly go offline again until the next day, or even next week. A single conference of this sort, once established, can continue indefinitely, as long as there are any participants left who still want it to. Since participants may be allowed to "come" and "go" at any time, this may be a very long time indeed!

Furthermore, if each participant keeps a copy of the messages that have been contributed, then everyone automatically has a complete and exact verbatim record of everything said. No stenographer, no secretary, no minuting—the record is there for free.

There is a technical term for a communication system where the communicating parties are not precisely synchronised with each other: it is called *asynchronous* communication. So I will call an electronic conference, where there is no required synchronisation between the participants, an *asynchronous conference*.

Of course, an asynchronous electronic conference is no substitute for traditional, face-to-face, meetings. For one thing, asynchronous discussions are obviously going to be *slower* than they would be in a real meeting. Also, because different people participate at different times to suit themselves, the flow of discussions may be quite disjoint. There may even be several different topics or "threads" being discussed simultaneously, though that is arguably a positive advantage of the asynchronous conference. But clearly, there will be circumstances in which asynchronous conferencing works well, and other cases where it works very badly: the trick, of course, is to apply it in just the right circumstances.

Asynchronous conferences, based on this sort of primarily textual messaging, abound on the Internet. There are literally tens of thousands of such conferences in progress all the time. New ones are being created (and old ones petering out) all the time. For the most part, these conferences are organised around specific topics or interests that people may wish to exchange information about. Given the global reach of the Internet, it is not surprising to find that there are dedicated conferences on a truly vast range of topics. Everything from the sublime to the ridiculous is out there somewhere. So whether your interest is in keeping tropical fish, the latest ways of applying technology in education, or campaigning against human rights abuses, there is probably a group of similarly minded people who would love you to join their discussion.

Many asynchronous conferences on the Internet are, quite literally, e-mail mailing lists. Some are managed just using the idea of MS-OE e-mail groups. As long as some one person takes responsibility for managing a master copy of the group list, and circulating updates, as the participants change, that can work perfectly well. Alternatively, the person managing the list can just hold on to the master copy. Any participant wanting to post a new message sends it to this person and he or she then forwards it to the rest of the group. This kind of basic e-mail based conference has the advantage that anyone can set one up with no special tools or expense, beyond a normal e-mail client and Internet connection.

Of course, if an e-mail conference gets to have very many participants - and especially if participants can drop out, and new participants join, on a regular basis - then the administrative load in manually managing and circulating the list of participants and/or forwarding messages may become onerous. In that case one can resort to some kind of software to automate some or all of these tasks. Two popular packages of this sort are called *LISTSERV* and *Majordomo*. These are complex packages, and *not* suitable for an Internet beginner to install or manage! However you may well find yourself wanting to join e-mail conferences which someone else has already established using one of these tools. You can do this by sending e-mail to a special administrative address. This is automatically processed by the program managing the e-mail list. The e-mail message will contain somewhat cryptic instructions to tell the program what you want to do (usually join or leave a particular conference).

You will generally find out about e-mail based conferences via Web sites which describe them. These sites will also detail the particular instructions for joining or leaving. The messages posted to the conference may be collected into archives which are accessible on the Web. This can be very useful, as it gives you a chance to sample the sorts of discussions or exchanges that are going on before deciding if you really want to join up.

Be a little careful of joining conferences that operate by e-mail. There is tremendous variation in the volume of messages handled by these conferences, depending on how many people are participating and how interested they are. The most popular conferences may distribute several hundred e-mail messages per week! This can take quite a while to download, and make it difficult to separate out your

Welcome Aboard

What Is This Internet Thing Anyway

Your Net Computer

Getting On-line

The Web

E-mail

Other Internet Services

Welcome Aboard

What Is This Internet Thing Anyway

Your Net Computer

Getting On-line

The Web

E-mail

Other Internet Services

"ordinary" e-mail. It is quite an unpleasant surprise if you are not expecting it. I recommend that whenever you join ("subscribe to") a new e-mail conference, you take care to check your e-mail more often than usual for the following few days, in case the volume of messages is too high. If so, you can leave the conference again quickly, before you are completely swamped.

In any case: the biggest single collection of asynchronous electronic conferences on the Internet do *not* operate via the e-mail service. These are the USENET *Newsgroups*. Don't be misled by the word "news" in "newsgroups": these have nothing to do with the colloquial sense of "news" as in newspapers or television news. The basic concept of USENET Newsgroups is exactly the same as e-mail-based conferences. They are a mechanism whereby groups of people, with some common interests, can pool textual messages, and thus carry on conversations and discussions. But the underlying technology is quite different and separate from the e-mail service.

Messages from USENET newsgroups do not arrive in your e-mail Inbox along with normal e-mail, and you do not post to newsgroups in quite the same way as you send e-mail. However, it is common for a single "messaging" program to support both e-mail and newsgroup services, and indeed, this is the case with Microsoft Outlook Express, even though I did not mention this explicitly when discussing MS–OE previously.

USENET Newsgroups operate via a network of newsgroup server computers. Your ISP will normally operate at least one of these, and so do many other organisations. There are now well over 25,000 newsgroups established on a global basis. Not all servers support all newsgroups. The administrators of each server decide which newsgroups that server will support. For each newsgroup that a server supports it will hold an archive of all postings to that newsgroup for a certain period of time. The time may vary from newsgroup to newsgroup, and range from as little as one day to several months or longer. When a message has been on a server longer than the specified archival time it is said to have expired and the server deletes it. This is essential because, with tens of thousands of newsgroups, the storage to hold all the messages would otherwise quickly exhaust the capacity of the server.

When you post a message to a newsgroup on a certain server, it is automatically passed on to all the other servers around the world that carry that same newsgroup. This propagation can take a noticeable amount of time, from a few hours to several days.

When you first start your newsgroup client it will query the ISP's newsgroup server for a list of supported newsgroups. Then you can pick out from this list which newsgroups you want to "join" or "subscribe" to. This just means that your client makes a note of the fact that you want to monitor postings to those newsgroups. Then whenever you connect, your client will download from the server copies of any new messages that have been posted to the group. Given that there are so many USENET newsgroups, the choice may seem hopelessly bewildering at first. If possible, ask friends or colleagues for advice on newsgroups that might be worth joining. You should also have a browse through the *FAQ* for any newsgroup you are thinking of participating in. FAQ (pronounced "fack") is short for "Frequently Asked Questions". A FAQ is a document giving a list of questions and answers about a particular newsgroup. The main idea is to discourage new participants from raising questions that have already been exhaustively discussed and answered. Actually, FAQs don't just apply to newsgroups: you will often find FAQs on the Internet for e-mail-based conferences, and on subjects that are not covered by conferences at all. You can find a large collection of FAQs at:

```
http://www.cis.ohio-state.edu/hypertext/faq/usenet/top.html
```

Because USENET messages will be regularly expired from your server, you may miss out on some of the messages if you do not connect regularly. Also, in the interests of speed, your newsgroup client may not download complete messages at first, but only message headers (giving the originator and the subject). Then, as you select specific messages, the full text will be downloaded. Or, while you are offline, there may be an option to select messages for downloading; then you can go online briefly, download all the requested messages, and hang up again, so that you can actually read them offline.

This separation between downloading headers and full messages is useful because you may be able to tell from the headers that you are not interested in seeing many of the detailed message bodies. But it also means that you can sometimes be disappointed. If you download headers one day and then go back to read the messages the following day, some of those messages may already have been expired!

I will not present any detailed instructions for using a particular newsgroup client here: see the online help of your particular client for further information.

While both e-mail and newsgroup style conferences are very widely used on the Internet today, a third alternative technology - for essentially the same purpose - is now beginning to be deployed. This is to present the interface to the asynchronous conference via a Web page.

Typically, there will be one Web page where you can enter textual messages for posting to the discussion, and another separate page which gives you access to view the accumulated contributions of all participants.

This technology has a number of advantages. Many users find it more convenient and friendly because it uses the same tool - the Web Browser - that they are already familiar with. It does not run the risk of flooding a user's e-mail mailbox like an e-mail-based conference. It only generates network traffic to service people who actually want

Welcome Aboard

What Is This Internet Thing Anyway

Your Net Computer

Getting On-line

The Web

E-mail

Other Internet Services

Welcome Aboard

What Is This Internet Thing Anyway

Your Net Computer

Getting On-line

The Web

E-mail

Other Internet Services

to read the messages, unlike the USENET system which generally propagates messages to a large number of servers regardless of whether anyone will ever actually access them. It is also generally harder for junk messages to be automatically posted to Web forums. Finally, Web-based conferences can be easier to initially setup and to administer than e-mail and newsgroup conferences.

I expect that the use of Web-based asynchronous conferences will grow in the future, although both e-mail conferences and USENET newsgroups will also be around for a long time to come. You can also enjoy the best of both worlds by accessing USENET newsgroups through a web interface via *Google Groups*:

```
http://groups.google.com
```

Come In For A Chat?

I have explained how the Internet can support Many-To-Many communication in the form of asynchronous electronic conferences. That is very useful up to a point; but it also begs the question, can we not have "genuine", synchronised, meetings over the Internet, where people can talk to each other in "real time"? Well, we can!

Again, a wide variety of techniques are being experimented with, so I will settle for a survey of the possibilities.

Note that, since I am talking about synchronised communications, all the participants must be involved at the same time - regardless of where in the world they are, or in what time zone.

The longest established technique here is a so-called *chat* facility. This allows for the exchange of short textual messages, typically just one line at a time. The best known and most wildly deployed system of this sort is called *Internet Relay Chat* or IRC.

IRC is again a client-server sort of service. So you must normally first acquire a suitable client program, and then use it to contact some server computer. The IRC service is divided into distinct "channels". Using your client you can contact some server and get a listing of the available channels. You can then "join" a channel. Immediately, you will begin to receive copies of messages that other participants are sending, as they send them; and if you contribute your own messages, they will be circulated to all the other participants also. Like USENET newsgroups, IRC messages can be automatically relayed from server to server around the world. So participants in the same channel can be connected via different servers. However, servers are grouped into a number of separate IRC "nets": channels are shared only within each net, not between them.

IRC servers may be public or private: you need specific authorisation to connect to a private server. Public server IRC has been fairly accurately described as the CB radio of the Internet. It is certainly an acquired taste. Most channels are pretty loose and unstructured. However, it is well worth dipping into at least once!

For more information on Chat services, check out the Google directory at:

```
http://directory.google.com/Top/Computers/Internet/Chat/
```

Small Expectations

Internet communication can be great fun, educational, and help you make contact with new friends from around the world. But you should be aware by now that not all Internet services are equal, and nowhere is this more true than in multi-user discussion forums.

Let's use "conference" here as a generic term for any kind of multi-user discussion forum, whether it's an e-mail list, USENET newsgroup, or IRC Chat channel.

Every conference in this sense has some nominal purpose, objective, or topic for discussion. Despite that, many conferences drift far away from the intended topics. Sometimes, great arguments can erupt, in which a large volume of angry and abusive language gets hurled around (so-called "flame wars"). USENET conferences are particularly susceptible to the circulation of junk (unsolicited advertising) messages. At the other extreme, there are also many "conferences" that are effectively defunct because all of the active participants (if there ever actually were any!) have drifted away for lack of interest.

Internet conferences are commonly "unmoderated", there is nobody in charge, directing and controlling the discussion. There are some conferences that do have a moderator. The quality of these is usually better, though this will, of course, depend on the skills and dedication of the particular moderator(s).

In short - like almost everything else on the Internet - the quality of electronic conferences is highly variable. So, if you find that a particular conference is not, after all, as useful to you as you had hoped, don't be too disappointed. Just move on and try another one, or even consider starting one of your own!

MUD On The Super Highway

Chat allows participants to exchange short messages to carry on conversations. More sophisticated systems may locate the participants in some kind of "virtual" world. For example, in the simplest case, there may be "rooms" that you can move

Welcome Aboard

What Is This Internet Thing Anyway

Your Net Computer

Getting On-line

The Web

E-mail

Other Internet Services

Welcome Aboard

What Is This Internet Thing Anyway

Your Net Computer

Getting On-line

The Web

E-mail

Other Internet Services

around between—meeting, and chatting, with different people at different places in this virtual world. The world may be further complicated with various kinds of virtual "objects" that you can interact with. These arguably provide a richer virtual meeting or conference experience. A common use for such virtual worlds is in distance education. For example, see *Diversity University* at:

> http://www.du.org/

These virtual world systems also merge with various kinds of Internet *game*. For example, one can play chess, or bridge, or a wide variety of "role playing" games of the *Dungeons and Dragons* variety. This general class of Internet service has an elaborate jargon of its own, including MUDs (Multi User Dragons), MOOs (MUD Object Oriented, whatever *that* means), MUSH (usually interpreted as Multi User Shared Hallucination!) and MUVE (Multi User Shared Environment). These are accessed with a wide variety of mechanisms, including Telnet, specialised client programs, Web based interfaces and, more recently, dedicated video game consoles with integrated Internet connections (which can also double up as general purpose Web TV devices!). For more information on these topics look at the Google directory at:

> http://directory.google.com/Top/Games/Internet/

Multi-Media Conferencing

Various products have recently been developed to support forms of Internet communication over and above the exchange of plain textual messages. These range from versions of conventional telephone service—but at much reduced rates compared to normal long distance tariffs—to audio and video conferencing, and the provision of computer interaction tools such as a *shared whiteboard*. The latter is a window in which participants can draw or display images prepared in advance etc. A copy of the whiteboard window is visible to all the participants. Whatever is inserted in the window by one participant is automatically relayed to the others.

Examples of products supporting this kind of service are Microsoft *Net Meeting* and Netscape *Conference*.

The bad news is that, in general, the quality of interactive (or "real-time") audio and video over the Internet is very unpredictable and erratic: the Internet was not designed with this kind of service in mind, and does not yet support it very effectively. However, this situation is improving, so that audio and video may well become more important Internet conferencing technologies in the future.

Rules Of The Multi-user Game!

In completing this very brief survey of multi-user services on the Internet, I will sound a minor note of caution. Regardless of the underlying technology supporting any public multi-user Internet service, you should be aware that you may be participating in a global forum with people from widely different cultures and backgrounds to your own. The potential for misunderstanding, or accidental insult, is very real. Before you get involved with any of these services, I strongly recommend that you first familiarise yourself thoroughly with the general rules or conventions for polite behaviour on the Internet, so called *Netiquette*. There are various online guides to help you here. I suggest *The Net: User Guidelines and Netiquette* by Arlene H. Rinaldi, at:

```
http://www.fau.edu/netiquette/
```

You should also, of course, read any specific information that may be available about the particular service or forum you want to participate in.

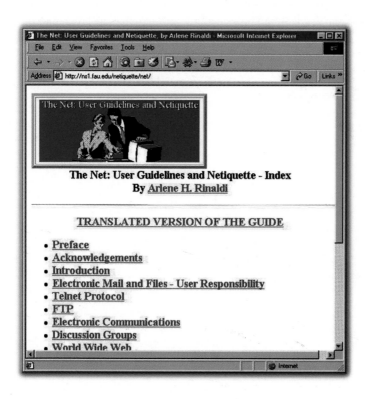

Welcome Aboard

What Is This Internet Thing Anyway

Your Net Computer

Getting On-line

The Web

E-mail

Other Internet Services

Bon Voyage!

I have given you a small glimpse of the variety of services - fun, educational, commercial, personal - that the Internet has to offer. New services and facilities are being introduced all the time. I hope you will now feel confident enough to branch out on your own. Again, don't forget to try out the *IOL* CD-ROM you received with this book.

Naturally , waiting for you when you do go online, there is also a Web site associated with the book. You can visit this at:

        http://www.iolfree.ie/~barrymcmullin/

Notice the special "~" character; this is called *tilde* and occurs quite commonly in URLs. At this site you will find links to all the web resources mentioned in the body of the book, together with some additional suggestions you may like to follow. If you have any comments or questions please do send them to me - by e-mail of course - at:

        barrymcmullin@iolfree.ie

I cannot generally respond to messages individually, but I will certainly incorporate suggested improvements, answers to queries etc., into the Web site and future editions of the book.

So good luck - *and welcome to the Information Age!*